PLAYFUL.LITTLE

paper-pieced
PROJECTS

37 Graphic Designs & Tips from Top Modern Quilters

Compiled by Tacha Bruecher

stashBOOKS®

an imprint of C&T Publishing

Publisher: Amy Marson

Creative Director: Gailen Runge

Art Director/Book Designer: Kristy Zacharias

Editor: S. Michele Fry

Technical Editors: Sadhana Wray and Carolyn Aune

Production Coordinator: Jenny Davis

Production Editor: Joanna Burgarino

Illustrator: Wendy Mathson

Photo Assistant: Mary Peyton Peppo

Photography by Diane Pedersen and Nissa Brehmer of C&T Publishing, Inc., unless otherwise noted

Library of Congress Cataloging-in-Publication Data

Playful little paper-pieced projects : 37 graphic designs & tips from top modern quilters / compiled by Tacha Bruecher.

     pages cm

  ISBN 978-1-60705-820-5 (soft cover)

1. Patchwork--Patterns. 2. Quilting--Patterns. I. Bruecher, Natasha, 1976-, compiler. II. Title: Playful little paper-pieced projects, thirty seven graphic designs and tips from top modern quilters.

TT835.P59 2013

746.46--dc23

                              2013017676

Printed in China

10 9 8 7 6 5 4 3 2 1

Contents

INTRODUCTION 4

FOUNDATION PIECING 5

Transfer the design • Basic foundation paper piecing • Freezer paper piecing • Choosing a foundation piecing method • Using the CD

Section One:
CALENDAR QUILT 13

A YEAR IN THE LIFE ... 14

BLOCKS AND PROJECTS

JANUARY—SNOWFLAKE 20
Modern Snowflake Table Runner, 22

FEBRUARY—SEALED WITH A KISS 26
Love Letters Journal Cover, 28

MARCH—ST. PATRICK'S DAY HAT 32
Irish Apron, 34

APRIL—UMBRELLA 38
Rainy Day Tote, 40

MAY—BICYCLE RIDE 44
Bicycle Basket, 46

JUNE—VINTAGE CAMPING LANTERN 52
Vintage Camping Lantern Pillow, 55

JULY—VINTAGE PORCH CHAIR 58
Vintage Porch Chair Cushion, 60

AUGUST—WISH YOU WERE HERE 64
Packed and Ready to Go Travel Pouch, 66

SEPTEMBER—AUTUMN HARVEST 70
Round Apple Pouch, 72

OCTOBER—HIDE AND SEEK 78
Halloween Boo! Banner, 82

NOVEMBER—THE SNOW BUNNY 86
Snowboarding Bunny Toy, 88

DECEMBER—LITTLE HOUSE IN THE WOODS 92
Winter Present Basket, 96

Section Two:
SMALL PROJECTS FOR AROUND THE HOUSE 101

KITCHEN

GRAPEFRUIT COASTERS Ayumi Takahashi, 102

LIBERTY STREET POTHOLDER Kylie Seldon, 104

TEA TOWEL Megan Dye, 108

KITE TOTE Charise Randell, 112

OFFICE OR CRAFT ROOM

NUTCRACKER PILLOW Chase Wu, 117

MAIL ORGANIZER Ayumi Takahashi, 120

ARTIST'S PORTFOLIO Cheryl Arkison, 124

SEWING MACHINE COVER Caroline M. Press, 128

COAT HANGER WALL ART Leila Beasley, 132

KID'S ROOM

CELEBRATION PENNANT Amy Lobsiger, 134

ROLL-UP BACKGAMMON BOARD Daniel Rouse, 139

KID'S BOOK BAG Laura Jane Taylor, 146

THE OLD CLOCK QUILT—LONDON TIME Lynne Goldsworthy, 151

THE CONTRIBUTORS 156

RESOURCES 160

Introduction

When planning projects, I have always been drawn to fairly intricate designs, and over the years, I have experimented with a number of techniques to achieve the results I want. Foundation paper piecing is hands down my favorite way of getting a grip on those little pieces and making sure my points stay pointy! I am very excited to have put together this collection of foundation-pieced projects from some of the most talented modern designers.

Foundation piecing can seem quite daunting, especially some of the more complex pictorial blocks. Such blocks can be made up of numerous pieces, which are difficult to keep track of. Then there are the dilemmas of which fabrics to use so the block has a modern feel and what to do with the block once you have made it! To ease you into paper piecing, I have provided an extensive introductory chapter on how to paper piece, and the individual designers share their valuable tips on how to use fabric placement and embellishment to give foundation and freezer paper piecing a modern edge.

The designs in this book range in difficulty and complexity. The calendar quilt is presented in the first half, with paper-pieced designs for each month, along with companion projects that use the same monthly design. Some of the more straightforward, geometric designs are a great starting place for getting your feet wet with paper piecing. After you are warmed up, some of the more intricate, pictorial designs will tempt and challenge you! And because sewing should serve a practical purpose, while also being fun, each paper-pieced design has an accompanying usable project.

Because foundation piecing can be a time-consuming process, the projects are mostly small and are designed to inspire you to consider how to include paper piecing in all your sewing projects. We want your paper-pieced projects to be finished and not relegated to the growing work-in-progress (WIP) pile!

Many thanks go to the talented designers who participated in this book. You all are a great inspiration to me, and I am very proud to have been able to work with you.

COMPILER'S NOTE

The online quilting world is a wonderful resource for inspiration and ideas. Below are some useful links to get you started. You can join and see what other quilters have done using the paper-piecing designs in this book, and also share your work. It's fun!

flickr.com/groups/
PlayfulLittleProjects

pinterest.com/ctpublishing

fatquarterly.com/books

Foundation Piecing

Foundation piecing involves using a paper or fabric foundation as a sewing guide and stabilizer to create a precisely pieced design. The term *foundation piecing* actually includes a variety of techniques that vary depending on the block design or the quilter's preference. The designs in this book use two techniques, with most projects requiring only the first:

- Basic foundation piecing

- Freezer paper foundation piecing

Each method has its advantages and disadvantages, and you can experiment to find what works best. You need not limit yourself to only one approach; in fact, some designs in this book mix and match techniques within the same block.

TRANSFER THE DESIGN

Regardless of the foundation-piecing method, you'll need to transfer the pattern onto your chosen foundation material. You can print designs from the CD directly from your computer onto regular printer paper or sheets of paper specifically designed for foundation piecing.

------------------ **TIPS** ------------------

In basic foundation piecing, the finished block will be the mirror image of the original design. With symmetric designs such as snowflakes, this is not important. And for some asymmetric designs, such as fruits or trees, the design might work either way, depending on your block. But in other cases, the reversal definitely matters; so, when making the letter N, keep this reversal in mind! The foundations on the CD included with this book are already reversed for you.

You can find a variety of foundation papers and freezer paper, cut to fit your printer, on the C&T website (ctpub.com).

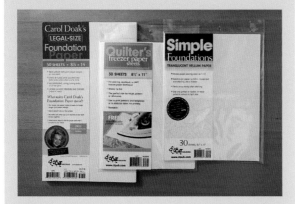

Sheets of newsprint, freezer paper, and foundation papers are also available on the Electric Quilt Company website (electricquilt.com).

When printing a design onto foundation paper, if Page Scaling is available in the Print Options, be sure to set it to 100% or None, to ensure that the pattern is printed without distortion.

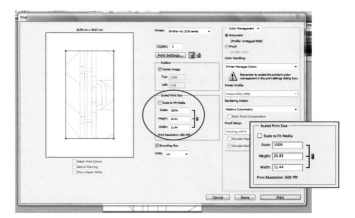

If you're not printing from a computer directly onto the foundation material, you can trace from photocopies onto the foundation using a lightbox or by holding the foundation and design up to a window. Before tracing, tape both layers in place to prevent either from shifting.

------------------ **TIP** ------------------

If you're using freezer paper, trace designs onto the matte side.

Trim the foundation, leaving ½˝ around the edge of the design. It is much easier to sew the design without excess foundation getting in the way.

BASIC FOUNDATION PAPER PIECING

In basic foundation piecing, you place the first piece of fabric wrong side against the unprinted side of the foundation, then position the second piece and line up the seams. Sew exactly on the line on the printed side of the foundation through the paper and the fabric layers. As you machine sew to add each piece of the design, make sure the right side of the design faces down.

Foundations

Foundations can be either temporary or permanent. Temporary foundations, such as vellum, printing paper, and freezer paper, are torn away after the design has been stitched together. Permanent foundations, such as interfacing, muslin, or other lightweight cotton fabrics, remain in place in the finished project. The type of foundation you use may depend on your finished project. Temporary foundations are great for avoiding bulk—for instance, when making quilts. Permanent foundations may be more useful when making very small pieces or when you want the finished design to be a little stiffer—for instance, when making bags.

Preparation

Make three copies of the design—one on the foundation of your choice and two on printer paper. One of the printer paper copies will be used as a cutting guide, and the other will be a master reference for piecing the design.

One oft-heard grumble about foundation piecing is fabric wastage. It is difficult to estimate the size of a scrap of fabric for an awkwardly shaped piece of the design.

Make an additional copy of the design to use as a cutting guide to take the guesswork out of cutting fabric scraps. For each piece in the design, cut out the corresponding piece from the cutting guide and lay it right side up on the wrong side of the fabric. Cut out the fabric, leaving about ½″ seam allowance all the way around. This seam allowance allows a little wiggle room for piecing, while also preventing fabric wastage.

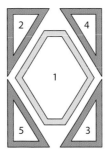

Paper-piecing foundations are usually numbered to show piecing order. The order is determined by the block's geometry, and there may be more than one possible ordering. In general, interior pieces are sewn first and larger pieces are added around them to build a design.

Some designs cannot be sewn using a single foundation because of their geometry. These designs are divided into sections that are paper pieced separately and then sewn together using conventional piecing. In this book, all foundation pieces are labeled with a letter for the section and a number indicating piecing order within that section. Designs requiring only one section will have only numbers.

Some designs can be divided into sections in more than one way. In this case, there is no right or wrong—choose what works for you.

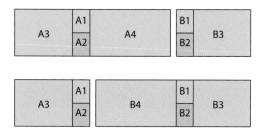

---------- TIP ----------

For a more in-depth look at how to divide block designs into different segments for piecing, refer to *Every Quilter's Foundation Piecing Reference Tool* by Jane Hall and Dixie Haywood (C&T Publishing, available as an eBook only).

Sewing the Design

1. If the foundation has more than one section, cut along the section lines.

2. Shorten the stitch length on your machine. A shorter stitch length (12 to 16 stitches per inch, or 2mm) strengthens the seams. Also, because each stitch perforates the foundation, a shorter stitch makes removal of temporary foundations that much easier.

---------- TIP ----------

Sewing through paper dulls needles quickly. Start each project with a new needle.

3. Use the cutting guide to cut a fabric scrap larger than the first piece in the design. Place the scrap on the back of the foundation, wrong sides facing, with at least ¼˝ seam allowance all the way around. Hold the work up to a light source to

check that the fabric completely covers the area. Pin the fabric in place or use a gluestick if the first piece is so small that a pin would be in the way.

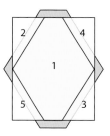

4. Use the cutting guide to cut a fabric scrap larger than the second piece. Line it up with the first fabric piece, right sides facing, overlapping the seamline by at least ¼˝.

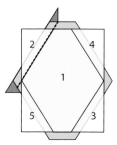

---------- TIP ----------

Before sewing, check the placement of each fabric scrap by pinning along the seamline and folding back the scrap to make sure it sufficiently covers the area. It is easier to reposition the fabric before sewing than to try to unpick the seam *without* tearing the foundation. Make sure the pin is out of the way before sewing.

5. Sew along the line dividing the two pieces on the front of the foundation. Backstitch at the beginning and end of the seam. Do not sew past the line at either end, unless the line runs to the outside edge of the foundation pattern, in which case sew ¼˝ into the outside seam allowance of the finished piece.

6. Trim the seam allowance to ¼˝. Trim now to avoid unwanted shadows later. The next seam will secure the beginning and end of this seam.

7. Fold back the second fabric piece and press in place.

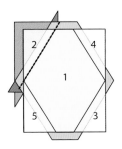

------------------ **TIP** ------------------

Important! Press after sewing each piece in the design to keep the block flat.

8. Add the remaining pieces in the design following Steps 4–7.

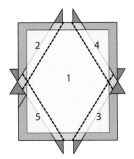

9. If the design was assembled in several sections, leave all foundations in place and use pins to align any seams and design elements that span sections. Sew the sections together and press the seams between sections.

When the design is finished, the pieces on the outer edges of the design should extend beyond the foundation by at least ¼˝. Trim the finished block to create an even ¼˝ seam allowance all around.

Foundation Removal

Start by removing the foundation from the last piece you stitched. To remove the foundation, first fold the foundation back along the seamline and crease well with your fingers. Then press down on the seam with one hand and carefully tear the foundation away with the other hand.

------------------ **TIP** ------------------

Tweezers can be very useful for removing stubborn bits of foundation papers.

FREEZER PAPER PIECING

In freezer paper piecing (not to be confused with basic foundation piecing using freezer paper as the foundation), each piece in the foundation is cut out separately and ironed to the fabric. Tick marks are used to pin-match seams and ensure accuracy. To make sure you don't sew *through* the foundation, sew the fabrics together using the edge of the freezer paper foundation as the sewing guide.

Several projects in this book start with basic foundation piecing, switch to freezer paper piecing to add a Y-seam, and then resume with basic foundation piecing for the rest of the project. For illustration purposes, we will use a paper piecing design and show how it would be done entirely using freezer paper piecing.

English paper piecing is similar to freezer paper piecing in that every patch gets its own foundation.

------------------ **TIP** ------------------

My book *Hexa-Go-Go*, published by Stash Books, is a great reference if you are interested in finding out more about English paper piecing and, in particular, hexagons.

Preparation

Make two copies of the block pattern. Trace one copy onto the matte side of freezer paper using a pencil, and print a second copy on regular paper as a master reference. Indicate on the master reference copy where different fabrics and colors will be used.

------------------ **TIP** ------------------

Keep in mind that the finished design will be the mirror image of the pattern drawn on the matte side of the freezer paper.

Mark the Pattern

Label the sections in the foundation and number the pieces in each section according to the piecing order. Number the master reference copy the same as the freezer paper copy. Mark section lines using different colors, using broad-tipped markers so the color shows on both sides after pieces are cut apart.

Tick marks are essential for ensuring that each piece aligns perfectly in the pattern. Arm yourself with a pack of color pens and make tick marks (short lines) wherever any two pieces join. Choose different colors for each join to avoid confusion when sewing the pieces back together.

Alternatively you could use different symbols, such as crosses or double lines.

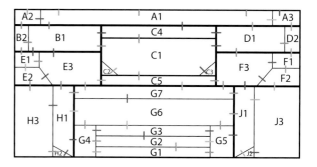

------------------ **TIP** ------------------

Use one pair of scissors for cutting paper and another for cutting fabric. Cutting paper dulls the blades more rapidly. Mark the paper-cutting scissors in a quickly noticeable way, such as with a ribbon on the handle.

Cut the Pieces

Using paper scissors, cut out one section from the freezer paper pattern. Cut out all the pieces in that section; then, lay each piece with the shiny side of the freezer paper on the wrong side of the fabric. Make sure to allow at least ¼˝ all the way around each piece for the seam allowance.

------------------ **TIP** ------------------

To avoid losing pieces or getting in a pickle trying to put the pieces back together again, cut out only one section at a time. If a section is divided into subsections, cut a subsection at a time.

Adhere the freezer paper pieces to the fabric with a hot iron. Use a ruler to measure a ¼″ seam allowance all the way around each piece; then, cut out each piece.

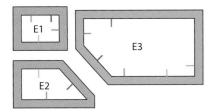

------------------ TIP ------------------

A Clover iron can help you adhere small pieces of freezer paper to the fabric and press the shape as you go along.

Some designs have very small pieces that can be difficult to handle while sewing. To manage such pieces, trace them onto a separate scrap of freezer paper. Trace all the relevant tick marks and add a ¼″ seam allowance to the freezer paper piece before cutting it out. Adhere it to the fabric, but instead of adding the seam allowance to the fabric, simply cut the shape directly around the freezer paper piece.

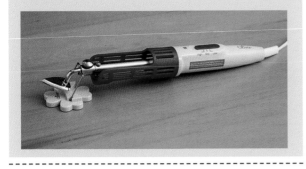

Add ¼″ seam allowance to freezer paper.

Sew It Together

1. Before you start sewing, arrange the cut pieces as they should appear in the section to avoid sewing the pieces together in the wrong order.

2. Reduce your machine's stitch length. Although you will not sew through the paper, you will need small stitches to make sure each small seam in the design is strong.

3. Line up the corresponding tick marks of two adjoining pieces. Place a pin through both marks perpendicular to the fabric. Holding that pin in place, use more pins to pin the pieces together. Pinning in this manner prevents the pieces from slipping and moving out of alignment.

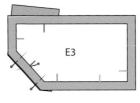

------------------ TIP ------------------

If the freezer paper pieces fall off during pinning or sewing, you can use your iron to adhere them again. Take extra care to make sure the piece is realigned in the right position. Use the ¼″ seam allowance and tick marks as guides.

4. Unless the adjoining pieces are part of a Y-seam, sew the pieces together from one end to the next using a ¼″ seam allowance.

If the pieces form part of a Y-seam, start and end the seam where the freezer paper starts—*not* where the fabric starts. Backstitch at both the start and end of the seam.

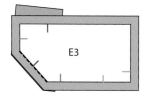

5. Press the seams before adding the next piece.

6. Sew all the pieces in one section at a time before sewing the sections together.

7. Remove the freezer paper.

----------- **TIP** -----------

For more details on freezer paper piecing, refer to *Ruth B. McDowell's Piecing Workshop*, published by C&T Publishing (available as a Print on Demand copy only).

CHOOSING A FOUNDATION PIECING METHOD

Basic foundation piecing is usually the faster of the two methods described in this book, because you don't need to cut apart foundations for every single piece. However, your choice depends on the design. If a design contains Y-seams, the freezer paper method allows you to maneuver better. If you are using slippery fabric, individual foundations make for easier handling, because the freezer paper acts as a stabilizer for each piece. Freezer paper piecing also allows you to control the pressing direction, which means you can press seams open to reduce bulk.

It is possible to combine methods within the same project to get the advantages of both. Several designers in this book have done exactly that: they use basic foundation piecing, switch to freezer paper piecing to complete a Y-seam, and resume with basic foundation piecing.

USING THE CD

The CD included with this book contains full-size patterns to complete every project in the book. The patterns are organized by project, so you can choose your project and get started!

Section One:
CALENDAR QUILT

A Year in the Life ...

FINISHED SIZE: 62″ × 90″ • BLOCK SIZE: 14″ × 19½″

ASSEMBLED BY Tacha Bruecher; QUILTED BY Angela Walters

This quilt is the perfect keepsake for your family. Have fun choosing fabrics, fussy-cutting motifs, and adding embellishments to each block to make the quilt more relevant to you and your family. The calendar panels are key to making the quilt look more like an actual calendar. They also are a fun way to further personalize the quilt—for example, by adding embroidery details to dates that are important to you and your family.

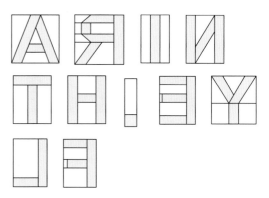

Materials and Supplies

Paper-piecing patterns are on pages CD1–CD3.

NOTE Refer to each month's instructions for fabric requirements for the individual blocks.

- **Black-on-white polka dot fabric:** 2 yards for sashing

- **White-on-white polka dot fabric:** 1 yard for right side border and cornerstones

- **Black text fabric:** ⅜ yard for letters

- **White solid fabric:** ⅛ yard for the month panels and optional ⅝ yard for the calendar panels (Refer to Create the Calendar Panels on page 17 for other options.)

- **12 fat quarters of coordinating prints** for month block sashing

- Freezer paper

- X-Acto or craft knife

- Sizzix Big Shot Machine (*optional*)

- Sizzix Movers & Shapers Base Tray (*optional*)

- Sizzix Movers & Shapers Cargo Stencil Number Set (*optional*)

- Stencil brush (*optional*)

- Fabric paint (*optional*)

-------------------- **TIP** --------------------

I used polka dot fabrics from the Spot On range for Robert Kaufman fabrics.

Cutting

BLACK DOT FABRIC

- 9 strips 2½˝ × 14½˝ to sash the blocks

- 8 strips 2½˝ × 20˝ to sash the blocks

- 2 strips 3½˝ × 53½˝ for top and bottom borders

- 1 strip 3½˝ × 84½˝ (pieced, for right border)

- 1 strip 4½˝ × 84½˝ (pieced, for left border)

WHITE DOT FABRIC

- 6 squares 2½˝ × 2½˝ for sashing cornerstones

- 2 strips 8½˝ × 20˝ to sash the word strip

- 2 strips 2½˝ × 60˝ to sash the word strip

- 9 strips 1˝ × 4½˝ to sash the letters

- 4 strips 2½˝ × 4½˝ to sash the words

FROM EACH OF 12 COORDINATING FAT QUARTERS

- 2 strips 1½˝ × 20˝

- 2 strips 1½˝ × 12½˝

- 1 strip 1˝ × 12½˝

- 2 strips 2¼˝ × 3½˝

- 1 strip 1˝ × 5½˝

WHITE SOLID FABRIC

- 12 strips 2˝ × 3½˝ for month number. Cut these after stenciling. (Refer to Create the Month Panels, below.)

INSTRUCTIONS

All seam allowances are ¼˝.

Assemble the Block

1. Assemble blocks January through December following the instructions for the individual months.

2. Trim each block to 12½˝ square.

DESIGN NOTE The calendar quilt is designed based on the seasons in the Northern Hemisphere. If you live in the Southern Hemisphere, you could rearrange the blocks or use a different fabric selection to represent your seasons.

Create the Month Panels

1. Enlarge a font on your computer until it is about 1˝ tall. Print a copy of the numbers of the months in this font. Place the freezer paper shiny side down on the numbers. Trace the numbers and cut out using an X-Acto or craft knife to create stencils for each month.

-------------------- TIP --------------------

The Sizzix Big Shot Machine, in conjunction with the base tray and magnetic number set, is ideal for making stencils for the month panels. Simply arrange the numbers on the base tray, place the freezer paper on top, and run it all through the machine. Quick and easy!

2. Iron the number stencils to the white solid strips. Use a stencil brush to apply fabric paint. Allow to dry before removing the stencils; then fix with an iron.

---------------- **TIP** ----------------

To produce sharp, neat edges, make sure the edges of the stencil are pressed snugly to the fabric. Apply paint sparingly to the brush, and use an up and down motion to paint the fabric.

----

3. Trim each number to 2″ × 3½″.

Create the Calendar Panels

The calendar panels should measure 5½″ × 9″, including seam allowance. You will need 7 panels with 31 days, 4 panels with 30 days, and 1 panel with 28 or 29 days. Various options are available for making the calendar panels.

1	2	3	4	5	6	7
8	9	10	11	12	13	14
15	16	17	18	19	20	21
22	23	24	25	26	27	28
29	30	31				

• Thermofax screen

Many companies can create Thermofax screens from photocopies or images. I used an A4 Thermofax screen to create the calendar panels. I used the same screen to print all 12 months. For months with fewer than 31 days, I placed a piece of freezer paper on the back of the screen over the numbers that I did not want to print.

---------------- **TIP** ----------------

Screenprinting is much easier than it looks, but not every print will be perfect. Always make more prints than you need to allow for ones that are flawed. Don't throw away flawed prints; you will be amazed how useful the numbers can be. I used the "flawed" numbers from one of mine on an advent calendar.

- ## Spoonflower

You can also use a fabric printing service, such as Spoonflower.com. If you arrange the image carefully, you should be able to get up to six panels from one fat quarter.

------------------ TIP ------------------

You can find my calendar panels in my Spoonflower shop: spoonflower.com/profiles/ natashabruecher.

- ## Commercial fabric

If you choose to use commercially available calendar prints, such as Kumiko Fujita's line for Yuwa, you may need to adjust the measurements of each calendar block or add sashing to the print to bring it to size.

- ## Replace

Instead of using calendar panels, you could replace the section with a stenciled word. For example, you could abbreviate the months— *Jan*, *Feb*, *Mar*, and so on.

Assemble the Calendar Blocks

1. Take a pieced month block and the calendar and month panels for that month. Sew the matching print 1½″ × 12½″ strip to the top of the pieced month block, and the 1″ × 12½″ strip to the bottom.

2. Sew the print 1″ × 5½″ strip to the left of the calendar panel.

3. Sew the print 2¼″ × 3½″ strips to the top and bottom of the month panel.

4. Sew the month panel to the left side of the calendar panel and sew to the bottom of the month block.

5. Sew the print 1½″ × 12½″ strip to the bottom of the block and the 1½″ × 20″ strips to either side.

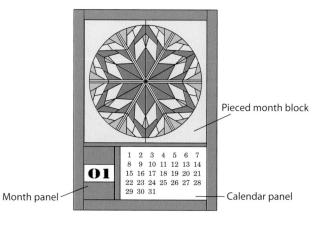

Pieced month block

Month panel

Calendar panel

6. Repeat Steps 1–5 for all pieced month blocks. Then remove the foundations from all the month blocks.

Sash the Blocks

1. Arrange the blocks in a 3 × 4 layout. Sew a black-on-white dot 2½″ × 20″ strip between the blocks in each row.

2. Create a sashing strip by sewing together 3 black dot 2½″ × 14½″ strips and 2 white dot 2½″ squares. Start and end the sashing strip with the black dot strips. Repeat this step to make a total of 3 sashing strips.

3. Sew the rows together with the sashing strips in between.

4. Sew the black dot 3½″ × 84½″ strip to the right of the quilt top and the black dot 4½″ × 84½″ strip to the left.

5. Sew the black dot 3½″ × 53½″ strips to the top and bottom of the quilt top.

6. Cut the leftover print scraps into 1½″-wide lengths. Sew the lengths together into a strip and trim to 1½″ × 90½″. Sew this strip to the right side of the quilt top.

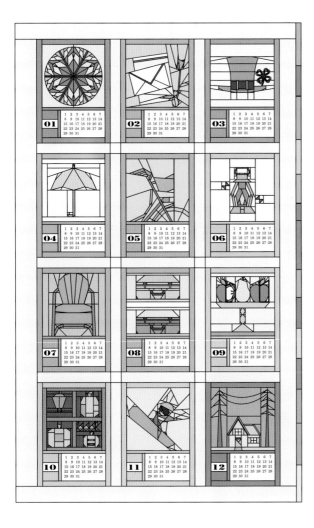

Assemble the Words

1. Use the black text and white solid fabrics to assemble 1 each of the Y, R, N, T, H, L, and F patterns; 2 of the A and I patterns; and 3 of the E and period (for the "...") patterns.

2. Sew the letters into the words "A," "YEAR," "IN," "THE," "LIFE," and "...". Sew a white dot 1″ × 4½″ strip between the letters in each word. Be sure to check that your letters are in the correct order before you start sewing!

NOTE The I patterns already include the 1″ × 4½″ sashing strip, so do not sew an extra strip before or after each I.

3. Remove the left white strip from the I in the word "IN." Sew the words together with a white dot 2½″ × 4½″ strip between each. Do not sew a strip between "LIFE" and "...".

4. Sew the white dot 2½″ × 60″ strips to the top and bottom of the "A YEAR IN THE LIFE ..." strip. The white dot strips will be longer than the word strip. Trim any excess.

5. Sew the white dot 8½″ × 20″ strips to the left and right sides of the word strip. Trim the strip to 8½″ × 90½″.

DESIGN NOTE When trimming the strips, keep in mind how you would like the words to appear on the quilt. Do you want the words starting at the top, in the center, at the bottom, or somewhere in between? You choose!

6. Sew the word strip to the right of the quilt.

Finish the Quilt

1. Layer the backing, batting, and quilt top and baste in place.

2. Quilt as desired. This quilt was quilted by Angela Walters.

-------------------- **TIP** --------------------

For ideas and techniques in modern free-motion quilting, see *In the Studio with Angela Walters* and *Free-Motion Quilting with Angela Walters*, both published by Stash Books.

3. Cut the binding fabric into 2½″-wide strips and sew them together into a continuous strip. Use the strip to bind the quilt.

Snowflake

PIECED BY Joanna Wilczynska • FINISHED SIZE of paper-pieced block: 12″ × 12″

This snowflake pattern is versatile; the sections can be pieced to create countless color combinations. This block is only one possible version. Challenge yourself to come up with your own snowflake pattern!

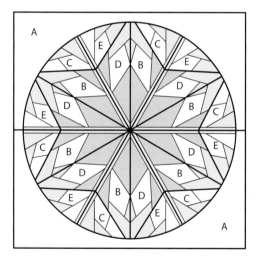

Materials and Supplies

Paper-piecing patterns are on pages CD4 and CD5.

- **Blue print:** 1 fat eighth for snowflake

- **Gray:** 1 fat eighth for snowflake

- **White print:** 1 fat quarter for background

INSTRUCTIONS

All seam allowances are ¼˝.

Assemble the Block

1. Trace 2 copies of section A and 6 copies of sections B–E.

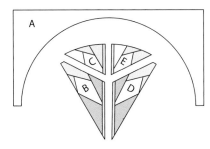

2. Piece sections B–E.

------------------ **TIP** ------------------

The snowflake pattern has 24 paper-pieced sections, 12 of which meet in the center. If you want to avoid handling so many points, cut off the ends of sections B and D before piecing. After piecing, appliqué an English paper-pieced hexagon over the center.

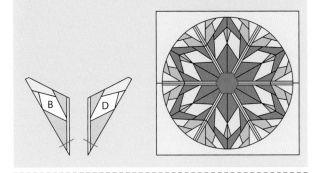

3. Join B to C. Join D to E. Join BC to DE. Repeat this step to make 6 BCDE units.

4. Draw around section A on the wrong side of the white background fabric and cut out, adding a seam allowance of ¼˝ all around as you cut. Repeat this step to make 2 section A pieces.

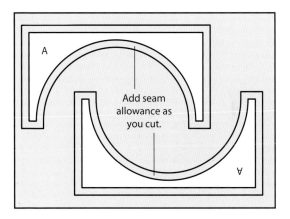

5. You have a choice for sewing the snowflake block together:

Sew the 6 BCDE units into a circle. Sew the 2 section A pieces together to form a hole, and sew the BCDE circle into the hole.

OR

Sew each BCDE section to a section A to make two half-circles. Sew the halves together.

6. Trim the block to 12½˝ × 12½˝.

Modern Snowflake
TABLE RUNNER

MADE BY Joanna Wilczynska • FINISHED SIZE: 16˝ × 37˝

Winter is a magical time of year, when the colors in the world seem to be washed away, except for the cold winter colors of gray, aqua, and off-white. BasicGrey's Blitzen Gray Grunge solid, Sketch Pool Screen Texture by Timeless Treasures Fabrics, and Muslin Mates White Snowflakes by Moda re-create that feel in this modern table runner—perfect for use during the winter months.

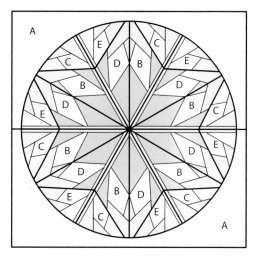

Materials and Supplies

Paper-piecing patterns are on pages CD6 and CD7.

- White fabric: 1 yard for background

- Gray fabric: ½ yard for snowflakes, runner, and binding

- Blue fabric: ½ yard for snowflakes, runner, and binding

- Backing fabric: ⅝ yard

- Batting: 20˝ × 40˝

Cutting

WHITE

- 1 strip 2½˝ × 16½˝
- 1 strip 5½˝ × 16½˝
- 3 strips 1½˝ × 16½˝
- 1 rectangle 3˝ × 6½˝
- 1 rectangle 8˝ × 6½˝
- 1 rectangle 7½˝ × 8½˝
- 1 rectangle 1½˝ × 8½˝
- 1 rectangle 2½˝ × 9½˝
- 1 rectangle 5½˝ × 9½˝

GRAY

- 1 strip 1¾˝ × 16½˝

BLUE

- 1 strip 3¼˝ × 16½˝

INSTRUCTIONS

All seam allowances are ¼˝.

Assemble the Block

1. Piece 3 snowflake blocks—9½˝ × 9½˝, 8½˝ × 8½˝, and 6½˝ × 6½˝—following the instructions for the snowflake block (page 21).

2. Sew the white 3˝ × 6½˝ rectangle to the top of the 6½˝ snowflake block and the white 8˝ × 6½˝ rectangle to the bottom.

3. Sew the white 7½˝ × 8½˝ rectangle to the top of the 8½˝ snowflake block and the white 1½˝ × 8½˝ strip to the bottom.

4. Sew the white 2½˝ × 9½˝ rectangle to the top of the 9½˝ snowflake block and the white 5½˝ × 9½˝ strip to the bottom.

5. Sew the runner together as follows:

- The white 2½″ × 16½″ strip

- The gray 1¾″ × 16½″ strip

- The blue 3¼″ × 16½″ strip

- The white 5½″ × 16½″ strip

- The 6½″ snowflake strip

- A white 1½″ × 16½″ strip

- The 8½″ snowflake strip

- A white 1½″ × 16½″ strip

- The 9½″ snowflake strip

- A white 1½″ × 16½″ strip

6. Remove the foundations. Layer the table runner, batting, and backing fabric and baste in place. Quilt as desired.

7. Cut the leftover gray and blue fabric into 2½″-wide strips and sew together into a continuous strip. Bind the table runner.

Sealed with a Kiss

PIECED BY Amy Friend • FINISHED SIZE of paper-pieced block: 12″ × 12″

February is the month of love. Even if you are not romantic, there is nothing more special than receiving a letter sealed with a kiss!

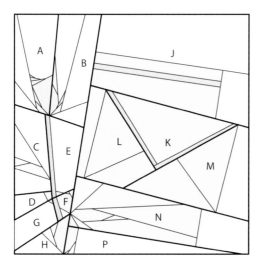

Materials and Supplies

Paper-piecing patterns are on pages CD8–CD11.

- **Background fabric:** 1 fat quarter

- **Assorted scraps** for envelope details and leaves

- **White fabric:** 1 fat eighth for envelope

- **Text fabric:** 1 fat eighth for letter

- **Red fabric:** 5″ square for rose

- **Ink pad** in poppy red

- **Kiss rubber stamp**

NOTE I used Kissing Booth by BasicGrey for Moda for this project because it includes small-scale text prints, textured solids, and Valentine's prints. I used a VersaCraft ink pad by Tsukineko.

------------------------------ TIP ------------------------------

It's always a good idea to stamp the fabric before piecing the block. Stamp the kiss onto the fabric intended for section K1 and heat set it by pressing an iron on the back of the fabric for about a minute. Assemble the block afterward.

INSTRUCTIONS

All seam allowances are ¼˝.

Assemble the Block

1. Assemble the left half of the block:

- Join section K to L to M.

- Join J to KLM.

- Join N to P to JKLM.

2. Assemble the right half of the block:

- Join section A to B.

- Join C to D to E.

- Join AB to CDE.

- Join F to G to H.

- Join ABCDE to FGH.

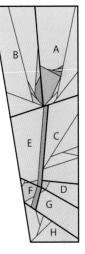

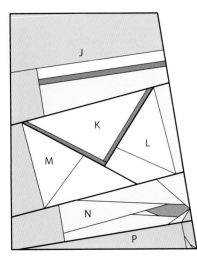

3. Sew the halves of the block together.

NOTE In paper piecing, you sew on the stitching lines on the *front* of the foundation. The sewn design is formed on the *back* of the foundation paper. This creates a mirror image, so the envelope in the finished design appears on the left side.

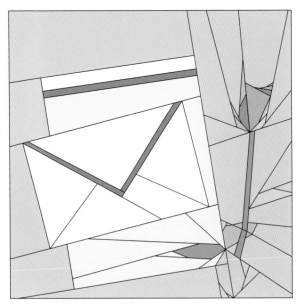

Love Letters
JOURNAL COVER

FINISHED SIZE of paper-pieced block: 7½″ × 7½″ • **FINISHED JOURNAL COVER SIZE, opened flat: 15¼″ × 10″**

MADE BY Amy Friend

This romantic journal cover, featuring the Sealed with a Kiss paper-pieced block, tempts you to write love letters. The cover fits a standard-sized U.S. composition book. It is quilted and lined, with sleeves to hold the journal in place, binding to frame the cover design, and a ribbon bookmark to keep your place.

Materials and Supplies

Paper-piecing patterns are on pages CD12 and CD13.

- **Pink:** 1 fat quarter for block background

- **Pink text print:** scrap at least 3″ × 9″ for bottom stamped area of front cover

- **Vertical heart print:** 1 fat quarter for back cover

- **Cream heart print:** ½ yard for lining and sleeves

- **Brown:** scrap at least 2″ × 9″

- **Assorted scraps** for envelope, letter, rose, and leaves

- **Binding:** ¼ yard

- **Fusible fleece:** 11″ × 16″

- **Button:** 1 for embellishment

- **Ribbon:** about 12″ long

- **Embroidery floss**

- **Composition book**

- **Kiss rubber stamp**

- **Alphabet rubber stamp set**

- **Ink pad** in poppy red

NOTE I used Kissing Booth by BasicGrey for Moda for this project because it includes small-scale text prints, textured solids, and Valentine's prints. I used a VersaCraft ink pad by Tsukineko.

write love letters

Cutting

CREAM HEART FABRIC AND FUSIBLE FLEECE

- Cut 1 piece of each measuring ½″ longer and wider than the book to be covered.

------------------ **TIP** ------------------

Use a measuring tape to measure the width of the cover. Start at the outside edge of the front cover, wrap the tape around the spine, and finish at the outside edge of the back cover. For a standard U.S. composition book, cut the fabric to 10½″ × 15¾″.

The following cutting directions assume the standard U.S. composition book size.

CREAM HEART

- 2 pieces 4½″ × 10½″ for sleeves

PINK TEXT

- 1 strip 2½″ × 8″

VERTICAL HEART

- 1 piece 8¼″ × 10½″ for back cover

BROWN

- 1 strip 1″ × 8″ for bottom edge of block

BINDING FABRIC

- 2 strips 2¼″ × width of fabric for double-fold binding

INSTRUCTIONS

All seam allowances are ¼″.

Assemble the Block

Make the Sealed with a Kiss block following the February block instructions (page 27). Trim to 8″ × 8″.

Assemble the Journal Cover

1. Sew the brown 1″ × 8″ strip to the bottom of the paper-pieced block.

2. Stamp the pink text 2½″ × 8″ strip with the words "WRITE LOVE LETTERS" and sew to the bottom of the brown strip.

3. Place the front cover fabric on top of the back cover fabric, right sides facing, and sew along the right edge. When opened, the front cover will be on the right and the back cover on the left.

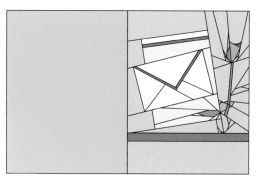

4. Remove the foundation. Apply fusible fleece to the wrong side of the journal cover.

NOTE Fusible fleece is great for keeping all the seams of the paper-pieced block in place and secure for quilting.

5. Layer the lining and the journal cover. Baste and quilt as desired.

6. To embellish, add a button to the brown band and secure with embroidery floss.

7. Finish a long side of each sleeve piece with a ¼″ hem.

8. Turn over the journal cover, so the lining faces up. Place a sleeve on each side of the cover, with the hemmed edges facing in. Baste the raw edges of the sleeves in place with an ⅛″ seam.

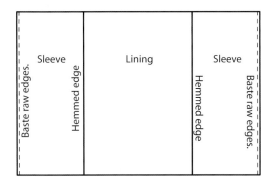

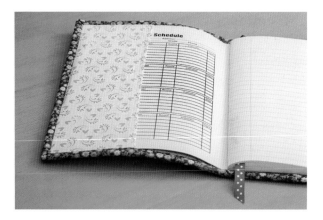

9. Secure the ribbon bookmark to the exterior cover of the journal with an ⅛″ seam—make sure the right side of the ribbon is facing down and centered at the top of the spine.

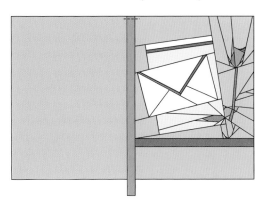

10. Prepare the double-fold binding as for a quilt. (Refer to C&T Publishing's Quiltmaking Basics at tinyurl.com/quiltmaking-basics.) Sew the binding around the perimeter of the front of the journal cover.

11. Hand stitch the binding on the inside.

12. Slip the composition book into the cover.

St. Patrick's Day Hat

PIECED BY Angela Pingel

FINISHED SIZE of paper-pieced block: 12″ × 12″

March 17 is St Patrick's Day, when people all over the world come together to drink, eat, and take part in parades. In Ireland, people traditionally wear a shamrock on their jackets or tucked into their hats.

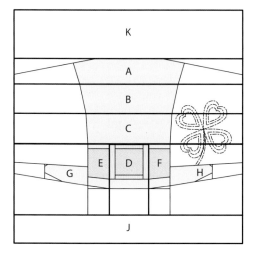

Materials and Supplies

Paper-piecing patterns are on pages CD14–CD17.

- **Gray solid:** 1 fat quarter for background

- **Green print:** 1 fat quarter for hat

- **Assorted scraps** for hatband (at least 2½″ × 6½″) and buckle (at least 5″ square)

- **Embroidery floss** for shamrock

INSTRUCTIONS

Assemble the Block

1. Assemble all sections.

2. Join K to A to B to C. Join G to E to D to F to H to J. Join KABC to GEDFHJ.

3. Trim block to 12½″ × 12½″.

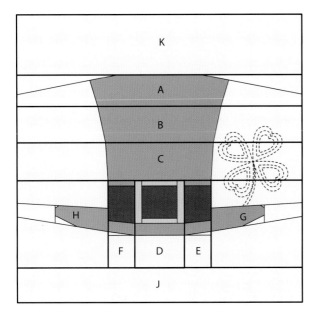

4. Using 6 strands of embroidery floss, sew the shamrock using a backstitch.

Irish Apron

MADE BY Angela Pingel • FINISHED SIZE: 23″ × 23½″, with 29″ sashing

This apron is perfect for entertaining on St. Patrick's Day! The sash is cleverly designed to look like a buckled belt, and the pleats give the apron a tartan flair. Pair it with a fabulous fabric and you have the recipe for a festive holiday. *Erin Go Bragh!*

Materials and Supplies

Paper-piecing pattern is on page CD18.

- **Print:** ¾ yard for apron skirt
- **Dark print:** ⅜ yard for sash
- **Mustard print:** Scraps for buckle
- **Paper-backed adhesive strip, ¼″-wide:** 2½ yards

MARCH—St. Patrick's Day Hat

SASHING

- 2 strips 3″ × 42″; then sew together along the short ends to create one long strip

- 2 strips 3″ × 40″ to sash the buckle

PRINT

- 1 piece 36″ × 22″ for apron skirt

INSTRUCTIONS

Assemble the Apron

1. Hem the bottom edge of the apron, if required.

DESIGN NOTE I used the selvage edge as the hem, as shown in the photograph on page 37. Selvage edges are so cute these days and can easily look like ribbon trim.

2. Fold the apron fabric in half widthwise, and press a small crease at the top to mark the center. Mark 3″, 6″, 9″, and 12″ from the center on each side.

3. Create the first pleat by matching marks at 3″ and 6″, right sides facing. Press the pleat so it faces the center, and pin in place.

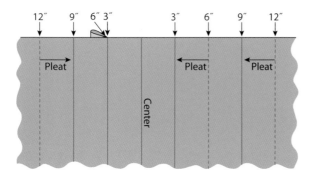

4. Create the second pleat as you did the first, this time matching the marks at 9″ and 12″. Press this pleat also toward the center and pin in place.

5. Repeat Steps 3 and 4 for the other side of the apron.

6. Baste across the tops of the pleats to hold them down. Topstitch 5″ down the inner pleats and 7″ down the outer pleats.

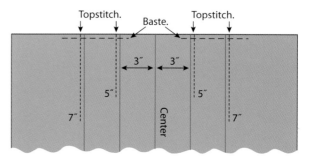

7. Hem the sides of the apron using a ¼″ double-turn hem.

8. Paper piece the buckle (page CD18), leaving a ½″ seam allowance on all sides.

9. Sew the 3″ × 40″ strips to both sides of the buckle using a ½″ seam allowance.

10. Match the center of the buckle strip with the center of the long sashing strip. Sew the long sashing strips to the top of the buckle strip, right sides together, using a ½˝ seam allowance. Remove the foundation.

11. Match the center of the buckle strip with the center of the apron. Sew the apron to the bottom of the buckle strip, right sides together, using a ½˝ seam allowance.

12. Press under the top edge of the long sashing strip and the bottom edge of the buckle strip (on both sides of the apron) by ½˝.

13. Apply the ¼˝-wide paper-backed adhesive strip to the turned-under edge of the long sash strip. Remove the paper backing and press the

long sash into place, over the turned-under edge of the buckle strip.

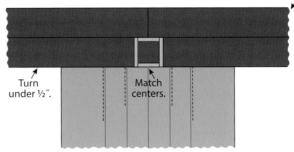

Apply adhesive strip to turned-under edge.

Turn under ½˝.

Match centers.

14. Topstitch the apron sash, including the buckle detail, from the front side of the apron.

15. To finish both ends of the sash, press and sew a ¼˝ double hem.

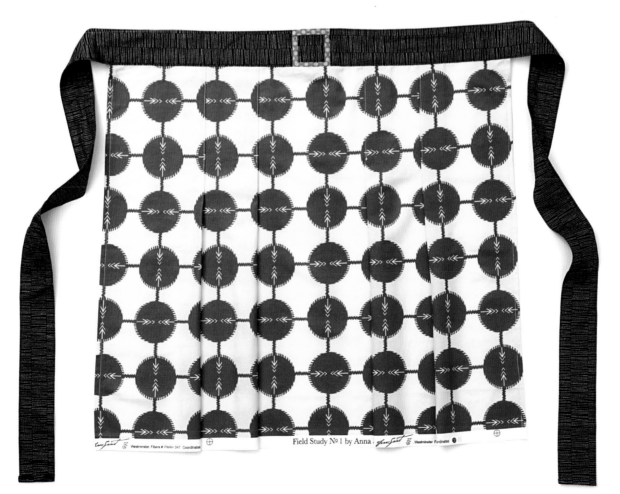

Umbrella

PIECED BY Leila Beasley • **FINISHED SIZE of paper-pieced block and sashing: 12″ × 12″**

Liven up those gray and rainy April days with this pretty umbrella! I used a vivid Liberty Lifestyle floral print for the umbrella.

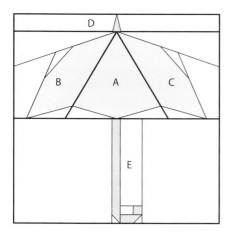

Materials and Supplies

Paper-piecing patterns are on pages CD19 and CD20.

- **Gray:** 1 fat quarter for background
- **Floral:** 1 fat eighth for umbrella
- **Black:** 2″ × 10″ scrap

INSTRUCTIONS

All seam allowances are ¼″.

Assemble the Block

1. Assemble all sections.

2. Join A to B. Join C to AB. Join D to CAB. Join E to CABD. Trim to 10½″ × 10½″.

3. Sew the gray 1½″ × 10½″ strips to both sides of the block.

4. Sew the gray 1½″ × 12½″ strips to the top and bottom of the block.

Cutting

GRAY

- 2 strips 1½″ × 10½″ for sashing
- 2 strips 1½″ × 12½″ for sashing

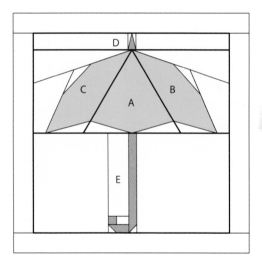

Rainy Day Tote

MADE BY Leila Beasley • FINISHED TOTE SIZE: 15″ × 16″

Tote bags are easy to make and so very practical. The main body of the bag is made using yarn-dyed Essex linen; Flea Market Fancy for the umbrella; a gray chevron by Moda for the background; and a fun, striped calendar print by Kumiko Fujita for the lining.

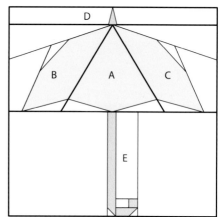

Materials and Supplies

Paper-piecing patterns are on pages CD21–CD23.

- **Paper-pieced April umbrella block:** for tote center (page 38)

- **Black linen:** ⅝ yard for sashing and for back of tote

- **Lining:** ⅝ yard

- **Fabric for handles:** ⅓ yard

- **Fusible fleece:** 2 pieces 15½″ × 16½″

- **Fusible interfacing:** 2 strips 1¼″ × 28″ for handles

- **Wool felt:** gray and white scraps at least 3½″ × 7″ for cloud and raindrops

- **Perle cotton or embroidery floss** in white or pale gray

BLACK LINEN

- 2 strips 3″ × 10½″ to sash the umbrella block

- 1 strip 2″ × 15½″ to sash the umbrella block

- 1 strip 5″ × 15½″ to sash the umbrella block

- 1 piece 15½″ × 16½″ for the back

LINING

- 2 pieces 15½″ × 16½″

HANDLES

- 2 pieces 5″ × 28″

GRAY WOOL FELT

- 1 cloud using the cloud pattern (page CD23)

- 2 raindrops using the raindrop patterns (page CD23)

WHITE WOOL FELT

- 1 cloud using the cloud pattern

- 3 raindrops using the raindrop patterns

INSTRUCTIONS

All seam allowances are ¼″.

Assemble the Block

1. Assemble the umbrella block following the April block instructions (page 39).

2. Sew the black 3″ × 10½″ strips to both sides of the umbrella block.

3. Sew the black 2″ × 15½″ strip to the bottom of the block and the black 5″ × 15½″ strip to the top. Remove the paper foundation.

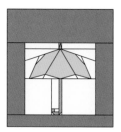

Appliqué and Embroidery

1. Apply the fusible fleece to the wrong side of the bag front and back pieces. Quilt, if desired.

2. Machine appliqué the clouds and raindrops.

3. Use embroidery floss to sew a running stitch from the bottom of each cloud to convey rain.

Make the Bag Handles

1. Fold the 5″ × 28″ handle strips in half lengthwise and press.

2. Apply the fusible interfacing to the wrong side of the strips, aligned with the center fold.

Fusible interfacing

3. Fold the long edges toward the center and press. Fold the straps in half again to enclose the raw edges; press.

4. Topstitch both sides of the straps ⅛″ from the edge.

Assemble the Tote

1. Place the front and back of the bag together, right sides facing. Sew around the sides and bottom edges. Turn the bag right side out.

2. Place the lining pieces right sides facing and sew around the bottom and side edges, leaving a gap of approximately 5″ on one side for turning.

3. Position the ends of the handles on the right side of the bag exterior 4″ from the side edges and 4½″ apart. Pin in place.

4. Place the bag exterior inside the lining, right sides facing, and stitch together around the top edge.

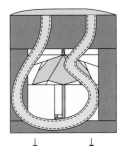

5. Turn the bag right side out through the gap in the lining and press the top edge of the bag so the lining sits neatly inside.

6. Topstitch around the top of the bag ¼″ from the edge.

7. Slipstitch the opening in the lining closed.

Bicycle Ride

PIECED BY Julianna Gasiorowska   FINISHED SIZE of paper-pieced block: 12″ × 12″

By May, spring has well and truly sprung. The countryside is a riot of color once again. What could be better than a lazy bicycle ride collecting flowers in bloom to adorn the kitchen table? The text fabrics used in this block were designed by Kumiko Fujita.

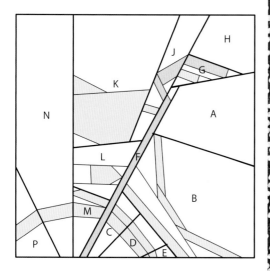

Materials and Supplies

Paper-piecing patterns are on pages CD24–CD27.

- **Green:** 1 fat quarter for background

- **Assorted red print scraps** totaling ¼ yard for bicycle, light, and basket

- **Fussy-cut flower scrap or appliqué flowers**

INSTRUCTIONS

Assemble the Block

------------------------------ TIP ----------------------------

Use the illustration below to help with fabric and color placement for the small pieces in the bicycle design.

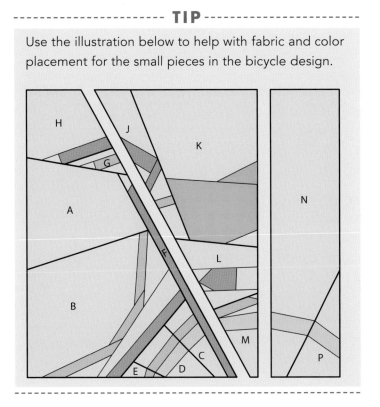

1. Assemble all sections.

2. Join A to B. Join C to D to E. Join G to H. Join J to K. Join L to M. Join N to P.

3. Join AB to CDE to F to GH. Join JK to LM. Join JKLM to ABCDEFGH to NP.

DESIGN NOTE Section K includes the bicycle basket and flowers. To appliqué the flowers, piece section K1 using background fabric; then add the appliqué. To piece the flowers, add background fabric to a fussy-cut flower scrap until it is large enough to cover section K1.

Bicycle Basket

MADE BY Julianna Gasiorowska • FINISHED SIZE of basket: approximately 14″ × 15″ × 5″

Add a vintage touch to your bicycle with this modern basket, perfect for both young cyclists and those slightly older ones who like a touch of whimsy. The basket is designed to be detachable and carried using a handle, which wraps safely around the sides and bottom when the basket is placed on the bike.

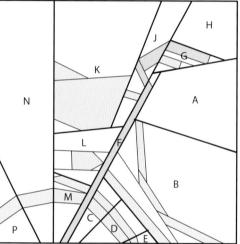

Materials and Supplies

Paper-piecing patterns are on pages CD28–CD38.

- **Blue prints:** total 1 yard for bicycle block background and basket

- **Lining fabrics:** total 1 yard (I used bright pinks and blues for contrast.)

- **Assorted scraps:** reds and pinks for bicycle

- **Fussy-cut flower scrap or appliqué flowers**

- **Fusible interfacing:** 2 yards

- **Batting** (*optional*)

- **2 buckles**

- **String or ribbon:** 1½ yards for drawstring

DESIGN NOTE To make sure the basket fits your bicycle, measure the distance between the handlebar and front wheel. Adjust the size of the basket by changing the size of the sashing strips around the bicycle block or by scaling the bicycle block using a photocopier.

BLUE PRINT

- 1 piece using template 1 for basket back, adding ¼˝ seam allowance all around as you cut

- 1 piece using Handle pattern (pages CD36–CD38) for basket handle, adding ¼˝ seam allowance all around as you cut

- 2 strips 2˝ × 12½˝ for sashing

- 2 strips 2½˝ × 15½˝ for sashing

- 1 strip 5½˝ × 38½˝ for basket bottom and sides

- 2 strips 3½˝ × 18½˝ for straps to attach basket to bicycle

NOTE Alter the width of the straps to fit the buckles you are using. The measurements given are for 1½˝-wide straps.

LINING

- 2 pieces using template 1 to line basket front and back, adding ¼˝ seam allowance all around as you cut

- 1 piece using Handle pattern (pages CD36–CD38) for basket handle, adding ¼˝ seam allowance all around as you cut

- 1 strip 5½˝ × 38½˝ to line basket bottom

- 1 strip 6½˝ × 41½˝ for drawstring casing

FUSIBLE INTERFACING

- 2 pieces using template 1, *not* including seam allowance, for basket front and back

- 2 pieces using Handle pattern (pages CD36–CD38), *not* including seam allowance, for basket handle.

- 2 pieces using template 1, including seam allowance, for lining front and back.

- 1 strip 5˝ × 38˝ for basket bottom

- 1 strip 5½˝ × 38½˝ for lining bottom

- 2 strips 3˝ × 18˝ for straps

INSTRUCTIONS

Assemble the Block

1. Assemble the block following the May block instructions (page 45).

2. Sew the background 2˝ × 12½˝ strips to the top and bottom of the block and the background 2½˝ × 15½˝ strips to the sides.

NOTE Join 1A, 1B, 1C, and 1D (pages CD32–CD35) to make template 1.

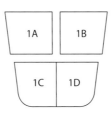

3. Center template 1 onto the bicycle block, pin or trace around the template, and cut out.

Apply the Interfacing

1. Remove the foundation. Apply the interfacing pieces without seam allowance to the wrong side of the basket front and back. Apply the interfacing with seam allowance to the lining front and back.

2. Center and apply the 5″ × 38″ interfacing strip to the basket bottom. Apply the 5½″ × 38½″ interfacing strip to the lining bottom.

3. Apply interfacing to the straps and to the handle.

4. *Optional:* Add batting to the basket front, back, and bottom. I quilted parallel lines on the front and back and left the bottom and sides plain.

Assemble the Handle

1. Place the 2 handle strips right sides together. Stitch along both long edges, leaving the short edges open.

2. Turn the handle right side out, press, and topstitch along the long edges.

-------------------- **TIP** --------------------

Add texture to the basket by quilting parallel lines along the handle.

Assemble the Straps

1. Fold the short ends of the straps, and then fold again as shown. Topstitch along the edges of the triangles.

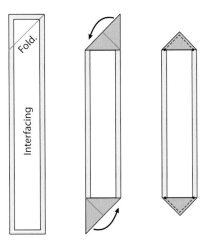

2. Press the seam allowance toward the center of the straps. Fold the straps in half and topstitch all around.

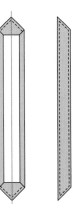

Assemble the Basket

1. Position the straps on the basket back as shown. Attach the straps by sewing rectangles about ¼″ and ⅛″ from the edge of each strap.

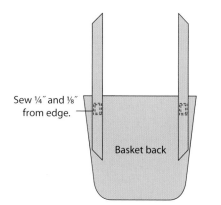

Sew ¼″ and ⅛″ from edge.

Basket back

2. Pin the basket bottom to the front, right sides facing. Stitch together around the bottom and side edges. Do not clip the fabric on the curves. Topstitch, if desired.

3. Pin the opposite side of the bottom piece to the exterior back piece, right sides facing. Stitch together around the bottom and side edges. Turn right side out and press. Do not clip the fabric on the curves.

4. Pin and sew the handle onto the right side of the basket exterior as shown, with the contrast lining showing as the handle goes across the basket bottom and up the other side.

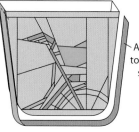

Attach to other side.

Assemble the Lining

1. Pin the lining front to the lining bottom, right sides facing. Sew from side to side around the bottom.

2. Pin the opposite edge of the lining bottom to the lining back, right sides facing. Sew around the bottom and sides, leaving a gap along the bottom for turning.

3. Finish the short edges on the 6½″ × 41½″ casing strip using a serger or by sewing a double-turn hem.

4. Fold the casing strip in half lengthwise and press. Fold in half again and press to mark a crease. Open the second fold and stitch along this crease to make the casing for the drawstring.

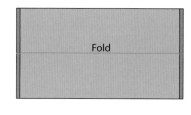

Fold

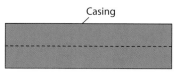

Casing

5. Starting at the bottom of the casing, topstitch along each short edge about ⅛″ from the edge and stopping 1″ from the bottom of the strip.

6. Separate the 2 layers at the bottom of the strip. Pin one of the layers around the top of the basket lining, right sides facing, with the ends of the casing meeting. Sew in place.

Finish the Basket

1. Insert the exterior basket into the lining, right sides together. Pin the open edge of the drawstring strip to the top of the exterior basket; stitch all round, making sure the handle is tucked down out of the way.

2. Turn the basket right side out through the gap in the bottom of the lining. Push the lining to the inside of the basket. Slipstitch the opening in the lining closed.

3. Press the lining so it is not visible from the outside and topstitch along the top edge of the basket.

4. Attach the buckles to the straps.

5. Thread the ribbon or string through the drawstring casing.

Vintage Camping
LANTERN

PIECED BY Tamiko Percell • FINISHED SIZE of paper-pieced block (includes bug strips): 12″ × 12″

Begone ugly, green lanterns. This vintage-inspired lantern is what camping dreams are made of. Text prints by Kumiko Fujita and Suzuko Koseki, combined with Liberty of London flowers and some polka dots, will make you wish fabric designers were in the camping business!

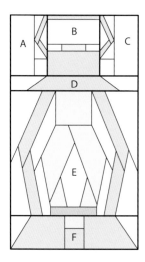

Materials and Supplies

Paper-piecing patterns are on page CD39.

- **Freezer paper** for piecing
- **Polka dot fabric:** 1 fat quarter for background
- **Liberty of London fabric:** scraps totaling ⅛ yard for lantern
- **Green print fabric:** 2 small scraps for button and lid
- **Blue text fabric:** 4″ × 4″ for flame
- **Yellow text fabric:** 10″ × 10″ for glass
- **Black-and-white print fabric:** 2 squares 2″ × 2″ for bugs

Cutting

POLKA DOT

- 4 squares 1¼″ × 1¼″ for bug blocks
- 2 squares 2″ × 2″ for bug blocks
- 1 strip 2¼″ × 5¾″ for top of lantern block
- 1 strip 2″ × 5¾″ for bottom of lantern block
- 2 strips 2″ × 2¾″ to sash the bugs
- 1 piece 4¼″ × 4″
- 1 piece 4¼″ × 7¾″
- 1 piece 4¼″ × 4¾″
- 1 piece 4¼″ × 7″

INSTRUCTIONS

Allow ¼″ for all seam allowances. Sew the very small pieces, such as the lantern handles, with a ¼″ seam allowance but trim to ⅛″ after sewing.

Assemble the Block

1. Assemble sections A, B, C, D, and F of the lantern block.

2. Make 2 copies of section E. From one copy, cut out E1–E7 as one piece. Pieces E8, E9, E10, and E11 all have Y-seams and can be added using the freezer paper piecing method (page 9). Trace pieces E8–E11 on freezer paper and cut out individually. Use these as templates to cut out fabric, adding seam allowances as you cut.

3. Assemble the E1–E7 section. Sew E8, E9, E10, and E11 to the E1–E7 section individually, starting and ending the Y-seams ¼″ from the edge (page 12).

4. Position section E1–E11 on the second copy of section E. Use pins to align the seams. Continue to sew pieces E12–E19.

5. Join section A to B to C. Join ABC to D to E to F. Press seams open.

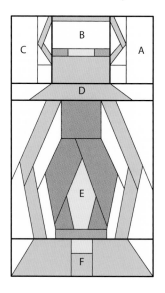

6. Draw a line down the diagonal on the wrong side of the 2 black-and-white print 2″ squares. Pair each square with a polka dot 2″ square and sew ¼″ seam on both sides of the drawn line. Cut along the line to make 4 half-square triangles and trim to 1¼″ square.

7. Sew 2 half-square triangles and 2 polka dot 1¼″ squares together to make a bug. Repeat this step to make a second bug.

8. Trim the lantern block to 5¾″ × 10″. Sew the polka dot 2¼″ × 5¾″ strip to the top of the lantern; then sew the polka dot 2″ × 5¾″ strip to the bottom of the lantern.

9. Sew a polka dot 2″ × 2¾″ strip to the right of a bug. Sew the polka dot 4¼″ × 7¾″ strip to the top of the bug and the polka dot 4¼″ × 4″ strip to the bottom.

10. Sew a polka dot 2″ × 2¾″ strip to the left of the other bug. Sew the polka dot 4¼″ × 4¾″ strip to the top of the bug and the polka dot 4¼″ × 7″ strip to the bottom.

11. Sew the lantern between the 2 bug strips and trim to 12½″ × 12½″.

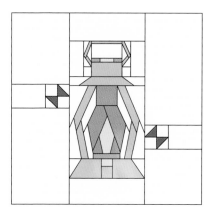

Vintage Camping
LANTERN PILLOW

MADE BY Tamiko Percell • FINISHED PILLOW SIZE: 18″ × 18″

Know any camping fanatics? Why not make them a vintage lantern pillow to snuggle up with around the campfire and to give their tent that warm homey feel.

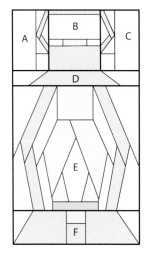

Materials and Supplies

Paper-piecing patterns are on page CD40.

- Freezer paper for piecing
- Polka dot fabric: ½ yard for background
- Scraps ranging from 3″ × 3″ to 10″ × 10″ for lantern, flame, glass, lid, and button
- Green print fabric: 2½″ × 2½″ for bug
- Backing fabric: 18″ × 19″ and 4″ × 19″
- 18″ zipper
- Lining fabric: 20″ × 20″
- Batting: 20″ × 20″
- Dark print fabric: ¼ yard for binding
- Pillow form: 18″ × 18″
- Black embroidery thread

Cutting

POLKA DOT

- 2 squares 1¾″ × 1¾″ for bug block
- 1 square 2½″ × 2½″ for bug half-square triangles
- 1 strip 2½″ × 3″ for bug block sashing
- 1 strip 2½″ × 5″ for bug block sashing
- 1 strip 3″ × 5″ for bug block sashing
- 1 strip 7½″ × 14″ for bug block sashing
- 1 strip 2″ × 7¼″ for lantern block sashing
- 1 strip 2″ × 10″ for lantern block sashing
- 1 piece 11½″ × 11¾″ for lantern block sashing

DARK PRINT

- 2 strips 2¼″ × width of fabric for binding

INSTRUCTIONS

Allow ¼″ for all seam allowances.

Assemble the Lantern and Bug Blocks

1. Assemble the lantern following the June block instructions (page 53). Trim the lantern block to 5¾″ × 10″.

2. Piece a bug following Steps 6 and 7 of the June block instructions (page 54) using the 2½″ polka dot squares. Trim the half-square triangles to 1¾″.

Assemble the Pillow Top

1. Sew the 2″ × 10″ strip to the right of the lantern block. Sew the 2″ × 7¼″ strip to the bottom of the lantern block. Sew the 11½″ × 11¾″ piece to the left of the lantern block.

2. Sew the 2½″ × 3″ strip to the top of the bug block. Sew the 2½″ × 5″ strip to the left of the bug block. Sew the 3″ × 5″ strip to the bottom of the bug block. Sew the 7½″ × 14″ strip to the right of the bug block. Sew the top section of the pillow front to the bottom as shown.

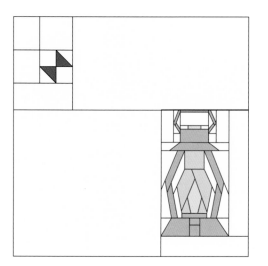

3. Remove the foundation. Layer the lining, batting, and pillow top. Baste and quilt as desired.

4. Hand stitch a flight path from the lantern light to the bug using a running stitch.

5. Embroider the bug's antennae using backstitch.

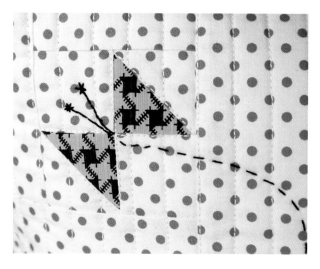

6. Trim the pillow top to 18″ × 18″.

Assemble the Pillow Back

NOTE For more details on pillow construction techniques, see *Pillow Pop* by Heather Bostic, published by Stash Books.

Finish the pillow back using your preferred method. I inserted the zipper along the longer side (19″) of both backing pieces.

Assemble the Pillow

1. Open the zipper. With wrong sides together, sew the pillow top to the pillow back around all sides.

2. Sew the binding strips together into a continuous strip and bind the pillow.

3. Stuff with the pillow form.

Vintage Porch Chair

PIECED BY Penny Layman   **FINISHED SIZE** of paper-pieced block (includes blue background): 12″ × 12″

Summer has settled in for the Northern Hemisphere. The days are long and warm, and the nights are short and sticky. It is the best time of year to pull up a porch chair, open a bottle of your favorite drink, and take life easy!

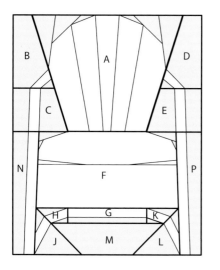

Materials and Supplies

Paper-piecing patterns are on page CD41.

- **Blue fabric:** 1 fat quarter for background

- **White solid fabric:** 1 fat eighth for chair legs

- **Assorted prints** for seat and back of 3 different chairs

TIP

Color a master copy of the pattern with the color of fabrics you wish to use to ensure that you use the correct fabric as you foundation piece the project.

INSTRUCTIONS

Allow ¼″ for all seam allowances. Sew the very small pieces, such as the chair rails, with a ¼″ seam allowance but trim to ⅛″ after sewing.

Assemble the Block

1. Assemble all the sections.

2. Join B to C. Join D to E. Join BC to A to DE.

3. Join H to G to K. Join M to HGK. Join J and L to HGKM. Join F to HGKMJL.

4. Join N to FHGKMJL to P.

5. Join BCADE to NFHGKMJLP.

6. Repeat Steps 1–5 to make 3 chairs total. Trim chairs to 4½″ × 5½″.

7. Choose the layout of the 3 chairs and sew them together side by side.

8. Sew a 4½″ × 12½″ background strip to the top.

9. Sew a 3½″ × 12½″ background strip to the bottom.

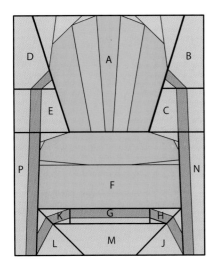

Vintage Porch
CHAIR CUSHION

MADE BY Penny Layman • **FINISHED PROJECT SIZE: 15″ × 16½″ × 2″**

Heavily influenced by her dad, Penny has grown to love all things vintage. This vintage porch chair cushion will take you back to the good old days when all the neighbors spent time sitting on their porches, rain or shine, waving at passersby.

Materials and Supplies

Paper-piecing patterns are on pages CD42–CD44.

- **Flower print fabric:** 1 yard for background and cushion back

- **Crossweave print fabric:** ½ yard for chair, gusset, and ties

- **Text fabric:** 1 fat quarter for chair arms and legs

- **15″ × 16½″ × 2″ foam cushion** (I used NU-Foam by Soft n Crafty, which dries quickly and resists mildew.)

- **Perle cotton**

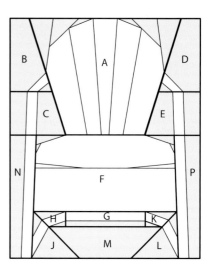

Cutting

FLOWER PRINT

- 2 strips 1¾″ × 10½″ to sash the chair block

- 2 strips 3¾″ × 15½″ to sash the chair block

- 1 piece 15½″ × 17″ for backing

CROSSWEAVE PRINT

- 2 strips 2½″ × width of fabric for gusset; sew together along the 2½″ edge to make 1 strip and trim to 2½″ × 63½″

- 2 strips 2½″ × 16½″ for ties

NOTE Change the size of the pillow to fit your chair by adjusting the size of the background fabric strips added to the top, bottom, and sides of the paper-pieced chair block. Cut a piece of background fabric for the back of the cushion the same size as the chair block.

To calculate the length of the gusset strip, measure the perimeter of the chair block and add ½″ for the seam allowance.

INSTRUCTIONS

All seam allowances are ¼˝.

Assemble the Cushion

1. Follow the instructions for the July block to paper piece 1 chair (page 59). Trim the chair block to 10½˝ × 13˝.

2. Sew a background 1¾˝ × 10½˝ strip to the top and bottom of the chair block and a background 3¾˝ × 15½˝ to the sides.

3. Sew the 2½˝ ends of the gusset strip together to form a continuous loop.

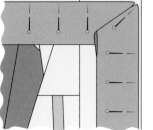

4. Pin the gusset to the cushion top, right sides facing. Curve the strip slightly inside each corner. Sew the strip to the top. Remove the foundation from the cushion top.

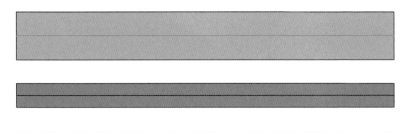

5. Press the ties in half lengthwise. Press each long edge in to the center fold. Press the center fold again so the raw edges are contained inside the tie; topstitch.

6. Position the middle of each tie on the gusset strip loop about 3˝ from each back corner along the side edges and stitch a rectangular shape.

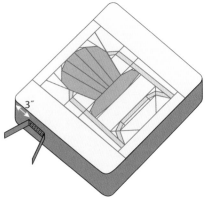

NOTE Adjust the positioning of the ties on the gusset to fit your chair.

7. Pin the backing piece to the other edge of the gusset, right sides facing. Sew, leaving an opening about 12˝ wide on the back edge for turning and to insert the cushion.

8. Turn the cushion cover right side out, insert the foam cushion, and slipstitch the opening closed.

9. Using perle cotton, embroider around the paper-pieced chair with a running stitch. Catch the foam cushion in your stitches as far as possible.

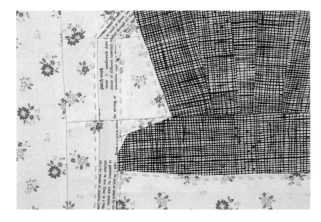

10. Use perle cotton to whipstitch around the gusset/cushion top seam. Hide the knot in the seam and bring the needle out of the gusset ⅜˝ from the seam. Take the needle straight above into the cushion top ⅜˝ from the seam. Bring

the needle out in the gusset ½˝ to the left of the previous stitch. Repeat, taking the needle into the cushion top straight above the last stitch into the gusset, keeping stitches ⅜˝ from the seam.

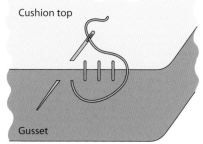

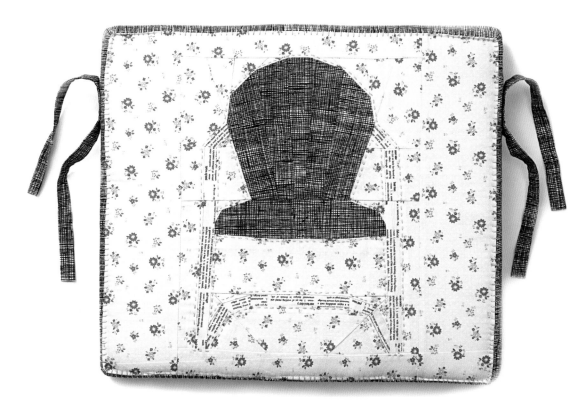

Wish You Were Here

PIECED BY Tacha Bruecher   FINISHED SIZE of paper-pieced block (including both suitcases): 12˝ × 12˝

August is typically the summer holidays in most European countries. Customize the suitcases to reflect where you've been—perhaps on honeymoon, a favorite vacation, or somewhere you are dreaming of visiting.

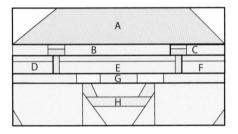

Materials and Supplies

Paper-piecing patterns are on page CD45.

- **Blue crossweave fabric:** 1 fat eighth for suitcase 1

- **Red crossweave fabric:** 1 fat eighth for suitcase 2

- **Mustard print fabric:** 1 fat quarter for background of suitcase 1 and lid of suitcase 2

- **Blue print fabric:** 1 fat eighth for background of suitcase 2

- **Red print fabric:** 2½˝ × 10˝ for suitcase lid 1

- White solid fabric: 1½″ × 12½″ for center strip

- Assorted scraps for suitcase closures, handles, and corners

- Fabric paint

- Scraps for embellishing: luggage tags and stickers

- Fusible webbing scraps to add embellishments

- Stamps and ink pad (such as VersaCraft) or fine permanent pen (such as Pigma Micron) for letters

Cutting

MUSTARD PRINT BACKGROUND

- 2 strips 2½″ × 5″

- 2 strips 1½″ × 12½″

BLUE PRINT BACKGROUND

- 2 strips 2½″ × 5″

- 2 strips 1½″ × 12½″

INSTRUCTIONS

All seam allowances are ¼″.

Assemble the Block

1. Make 2 copies of the suitcase foundation (page CD45). Assemble all sections. Sew the sections together. Trim each suitcase block to 5″ × 8¾″.

2. Sew a 2½″ × 5″ strip to the left and right and a 1″ × 12½″ strip to the top and bottom. Trim each suitcase block to 6″ × 12½″.

3. Stamp a holiday saying on the white strip of fabric, such as "Wish you were here!" or "We're all going on a summer holiday!"

4. Sew the white strip between the two suitcase blocks.

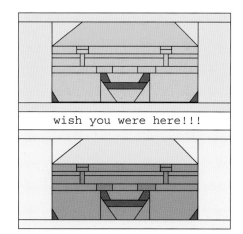

5. Use scraps to embellish the suitcases. Cut out label shapes from scraps and adhere these to the block using fusible webbing. Be creative and make some luggage stickers for your suitcases. Use fabric paint to draw flags of the countries you have visited or want to visit. Or add a little embroidery.

Packed and Ready to Go

TRAVEL POUCH

MADE BY Tacha Bruecher • **FINISHED SIZE: 4¼″ × 8″**

No holiday is complete without sunglasses. In fact, to make sure you don't forget to pack your pair of sunglasses, why not make them a suitcase of their own? The suitcase block is perfect for fussy cutting and personalizing to suit your style.

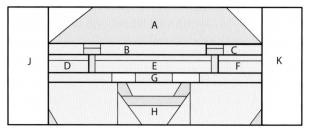

Materials and Supplies

Paper-piecing patterns are on page CD46.

- **Gray print fabric:** 10″ square for main part of suitcase

- **Blue dot fabric:** 1 fat eighth for background of suitcase

- **Fussy text fabric:** scrap at least 2½″ × 10″ for top of suitcase

- **Assorted scraps** for suitcase handles, closures, corners, stickers, and tags

- **Chevron print fabric:** scrap for back

- **Text print fabric:** 1 fat eighth for lining

- **Green text fabric:** scraps for flexible pouch clasp

- **Fusible lightweight interfacing:** 1 fat eighth

- **4″ flex frame closure**

- **Pliers** for flex frame pin

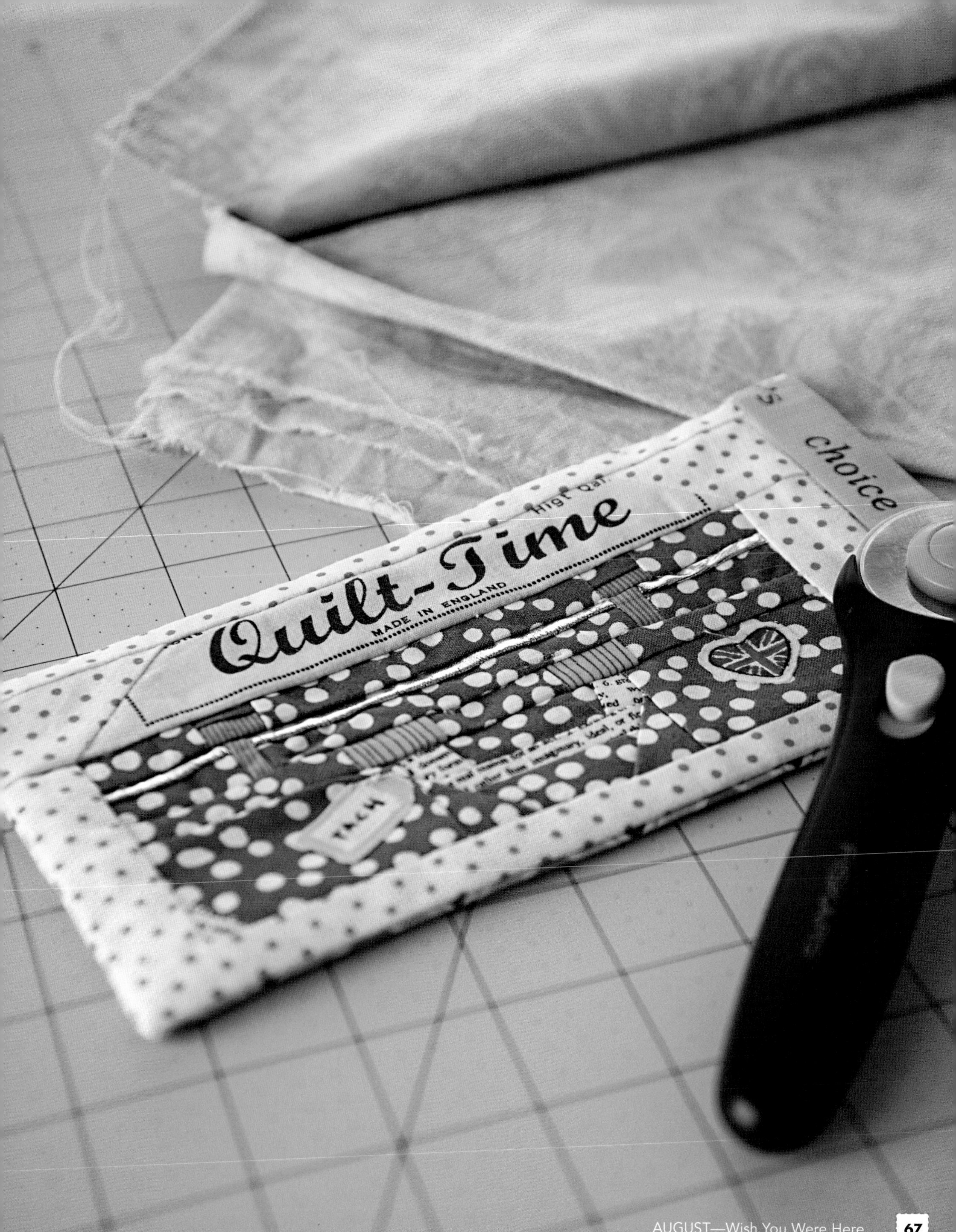
choice
Quilt-Time
MADE IN ENGLAND

Cutting

BLUE DOT FABRIC

- 2 strips 1¼˝ × 8⅞˝

CHEVRON PRINT FABRIC

- 1 rectangle 4¾˝ × 8½˝

TEXT PRINT FABRIC

- 2 rectangles 4¾˝ × 8½˝

GREEN TEXT FABRIC

- 2 rectangles 2˝ × 5¼˝

FUSIBLE LIGHTWEIGHT INTERFACING

- 2 rectangles 4¾˝ × 8½˝

INSTRUCTIONS

All seam allowances are ¼˝.

Assemble the Block

1. Assemble the suitcase block following the August block instructions (page 65).

2. Add blue dot strips 1¼˝ × 8⅞˝ to the top and bottom. Trim the block to 4¾˝ × 8½˝.

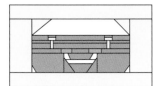

Assemble the Pouch

1. Remove the paper foundation. Apply the interfacing to the wrong side of the front and back.

2. Sew a ¼˝ double hem on both short ends of the green text pieces; topstitch. The green pieces should now measure 2˝ × 4¼˝.

3. Center the green pieces on top of the lining pieces, right sides facing, and sew. There should be a ¼˝ gap on both ends.

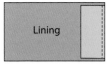

4. Center the opposite sides of the green pieces on top of the front and back pieces and sew in place. There should be a ¼˝ gap on both ends.

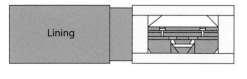

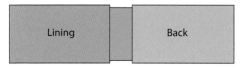

5. Pin the front to the back, right sides facing, and sew along the bottom and sides.

6. Pin the lining front to the lining back, right sides facing, and sew along all edges, leaving a gap in the bottom for turning. Remove the foundation.

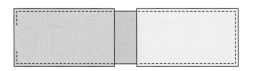

7. Turn the pouch right side out. Press so that the green top pieces are folded in half. Stitch the opening in the bottom of the lining closed.

8. Topstitch all the way around the top of the pouch, just under the green text top pieces, to form a casing for the flex frame closure.

9. Insert the flex frame closure through the casing.

Autumn Harvest

PIECED BY Charise Randell • FINISHED SIZE of paper-pieced block: 12″ × 12″

This block is inspired by fall's bounty of fruit displayed on a stylish fruit stand. Have fun picking fabrics to make this block fun and whimsical. Fabrics used in this block include Apple of My Eye from Riley Blake, prints by Suzuko Koseki for Yuwa, a text print by Kumiko Fujita for Yuwa, and Denyse Schmidt prints.

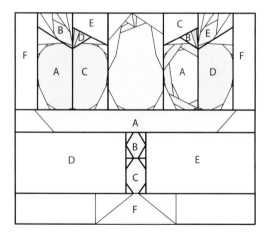

Materials and Supplies

Paper-piecing patterns are on page CD47–CD49.

- **Freezer paper** for piecing the pear
- **Red print fabrics:** 3 squares 5″ × 5″ and 7 scraps 2½″ × 1″ for apples
- **White print fabric:** 2¼″ × 3½″ for inside of left apple
- **Green fabric:** 2 pieces 1¼″ × 2¼″ for leaves
- **Brown fabric:** 2 pieces 1″ × 2″ for stems
- **Polka dot background fabric:** 1 fat quarter
- **Blue text fabric:** 1¾″ × 11″ for top of fruit stand
- **Blue print fabric:** 2″ × 4½″, 1½″ × 1¾″, and 1½″ × 2¼″ for base of fruit stand
- **Yellow print fabric:** 1⅝″ × 12½″ for tablecloth

INSTRUCTIONS

Assemble the Block

1. Assemble the sections for the left apple. Join section A to B. Join C to AB. Join D to E. Join F to DE. Join ABC to DEF.

2. Assemble the sections for the right apple. Join section A to B. Join F to AB. Join C to D. Join E to CD. Join ABF to CDE.

------------------- **TIP** -------------------

Work on each apple separately. Many pieces look similar, but they are mirror images. So piece each apple separately to stay organized.

3. The pear contains 2 Y-seams that are best done using freezer paper foundations. Trace pieces 7 and 8 onto the matte side of freezer

paper and cut out the patterns. Press the patterns onto the wrong side of the fabric and cut out, adding seam allowances as you cut.

4. Make 2 copies of the pear foundation. From one copy, cut pieces 1–6 as a single piece (do not cut apart each piece) and assemble. Cut out pieces 7 and 8 individually, and add them using the freezer paper method (page 9) to handle Y-seams. Pin sewn pieces 1–8 onto the second copy, align seams, and continue piecing the rest of the pear.

5. Stitch the left apple to the pear. Stitch the left apple/pear to the right apple.

6. Assemble each section of the fruit stand. Join B to C. Join D to BC to E. Join A to DBCE to F.

7. Stitch the left apple, right apple, and pear to the fruit stand.

8. Cut a polka dot 1⅝″ × 12½″ strip and stitch it to the top of the block.

9. Stitch the yellow print 1⅝″ × 12½″ strip to the bottom of the block.

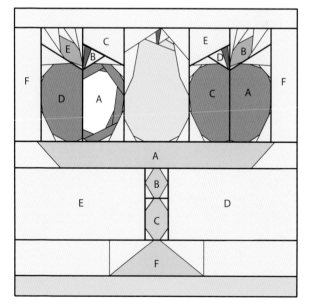

Round Apple Pouch

MADE BY Charise Randell • **FINISHED SIZE: 6¾″ × 6¾″, with a 1½″ gusset**

This adorable pouch uses the apples from the September Autumn Harvest block (page 70) as its centerpiece. A bright red zipper and red piping add extra fun details. This pouch is big enough for a take-along sewing pouch or for your makeup essentials.

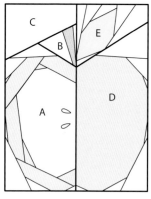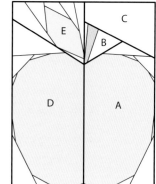

Materials and Supplies

Paper-piecing patterns are on pages CD50–CD51.

- **Red print fabrics:** 3 squares 5″ × 5″ and 7 scraps 1″ × 2½″ for apples

- **White print fabric:** 4″ square for inside of apple

- **Green fabric:** 2 pieces 1½″ × 2½″ for leaves

- **Brown fabric:** 2 pieces 1″ × 2″ for stems

- **Polka dot background fabric:** 1 fat quarter or ¼ yard

- **Lining fabric:** 1 fat quarter or ¼ yard

- **Binding and piping:** 1 pack of ½″ double-fold bias binding and 1 pack of ³⁄₁₆″ piping *OR* ½ yard fabric to make your own

- **Batting:** ¼ yard

- **12″ zipper**

- **Decorative zipper pull** (*optional*)

- **Water-soluble fabric marker or chalk**

- **Basting spray**

- **1″ bias tape maker** (*optional*)

- **⅛″ cording:** 1⅓ yard, if making your own piping

NOTE Fabrics used include prints by Suzuko Koseki for Yuwa, Sweet Shoppe from Benartex, and Swell from Moda.

Cutting

BACKGROUND

- 4 strips 1¾″ × 4½″ for apple border
- 4 strips 2½″ × 8″ for apple border
- 1 strip 2¼″ × 14¼″ for bottom gusset
- 2 strips 1¼″ × 9½″ for top gusset

LINING

- 2 squares 8″ × 8″
- 1 strip 2¼″ × 14¼″ for bottom gusset
- 2 strips 1¼″ × 9½″ for top gusset

BATTING

- 2 squares 8″ × 8″
- 1 strip 2¼″ × 14¼″ for bottom gusset
- 2 strips 1¼″ × 9½″ for top gusset

BINDING

- 2 strips 1⅞″ × 25″ on the bias for double-fold binding (if not using ready-made binding)

PIPING FABRIC

- 2 strips 1″ × 25″ on the bias for piping (if not using ready-made piping)

INSTRUCTIONS

All seam allowances are ⅜″, unless otherwise noted.

Assemble the Block

1. Assemble both apple blocks following the September block instructions (page 71). Trim, leaving a ¼″ seam allowance all around.

2. Use a lazy daisy stitch to embroider the seeds on apple 1.

-------------------- **TIP** --------------------

Judith Baker Montano's *Embroidery & Crazy Quilt Stitch Guide* is an app for learning embroidery stitches. It is available from iTunes, Google Play, and the Amazon Appstore.

Assemble the Front and Back

1. Use a ¼″ seam allowance to sew the background 1¾″ × 4½″ strips to the top and bottom of each apple block. Sew the background 2½″ × 8″ strips to the sides of each apple block.

2. Remove the foundations. Layer the 8″ lining square wrong side up, the 8″ batting square, and 1 apple block right side up; baste.

3. Edgestitch around the apple, leaf, and stem. Echo quilt ⅛″–¼″ away from the edge stitching.

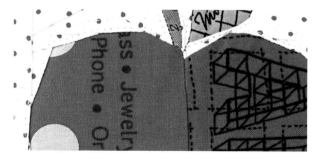

Assemble the Gusset

4. Center the pouch pattern on top of the apple; trace, marking notches for the gusset seams, center top, and center bottom. Baste ¼″ inside the circle and cut out.

5. Repeat Steps 2–4 for the second apple block.

1. Pin the zipper on a top gusset lining strip 1¼″ × 9½″, right side up for both, with the zipper stop ½″ from the end of the lining strip. Place a top gusset strip 1¼″ × 9½″, wrong side up, on top of the zipper. Baste ¼″ from the edge.

2. Place a top gusset batting strip on the top gusset from Step 1. Stitch all layers together with a ¼″ seam allowance.

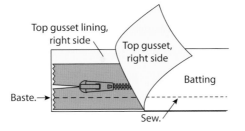

3. Press the top gusset and lining strips away from the zipper. Machine quilt the layers with lines ¼″ apart.

4. Shorten the zipper by stitching over the zipper ¼˝ from the end of the gusset. Use a wide zigzag on your sewing machine, or stitch a wide bar tack by hand. Trim the zipper and sew a bar tack ⅜˝ above the zipper pull.

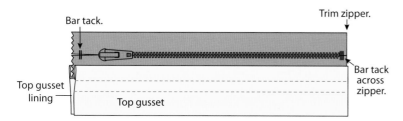

5. Repeat Steps 1–3 for the remaining top gusset lining, top gusset, and batting strips on the opposite side of the zipper to complete the top gusset.

6. Place the bottom gusset batting strip on the wrong side of the bottom gusset 2¼˝ × 14¼˝. Baste around the perimeter to make the bottom gusset.

7. Place the bottom gusset on the top gusset, right sides facing. Place the bottom gusset lining strip 2¼˝ × 14¼˝, right side up, under the top gusset. Stitch along both short edges with a ⅜˝ seam allowance.

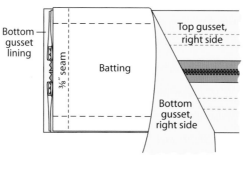

8. Turn right side out and press. Check to make sure the gusset fits the pouch. Fold the gusset in half, matching gusset seams. Mark the center of the top and bottom gussets. Test the gusset size by pinning a pouch panel to the gusset, matching the seams. If the gusset does not fit the pouch, restitch the seam, joining the top and bottom gussets to make the gusset larger or smaller. Once you have the correct fit, unpin the gusset from the pouch panel.

9. Machine quilt the bottom gusset layers together with vertical lines ¼˝ apart.

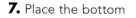

Finish the Pouch

1. Use a zipper foot to add piping to the front and back pouch panels, stitching ⅜″ from edge.

------------------ **TIP** ------------------

For a great tutorial for making and applying your piping, visit SewMamaSew.com > Learn > Sewing Tutorials > Pillows > How to Add Piping to a Pillow.

2. Pin the gusset to a pouch panel, right sides facing and notches matching. With the zipper open, stitch around the perimeter with a ⅜″ seam allowance. Repeat this step for the other side.

3. Fold under ⅜″ at the start of the bias binding. Pin the raw edge of the binding around the inside seam on the front of the pouch and stitch. Repeat this step for the inside seam on the back of the pouch.

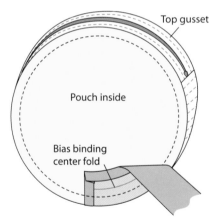

4. Fold the bias tape over each seam and slipstitch in place. Turn pouch right side out through the open zipper.

------------------ **TIP** ------------------

To make bias tape, fold the 1⅞″ strip in half. Press. Fold the long raw edges to meet the center crease. Press. Fold the bias tape in half. Press. Or use a bias tape maker and follow the manufacturer's instructions.

Hide and Seek

PIECED BY Kerry Green • **FINISHED SIZE** of paper-pieced block (including brown sashing): 12˝ × 12˝

October is the month of harvest and Halloween. You can play around with the four blocks that make up this design and devise your own hide-and-seek arrangement.

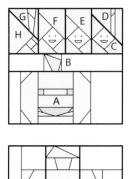
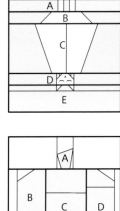

Materials and Supplies

Paper-piecing patterns are on pages CD52 and CD53.

- Orange print fabrics: variety to total ¼ yard for pumpkins

- Black print fabric: variety to total ¼ yard for background

- Green print fabrics: scraps for pumpkin stalks

- Gray prints: assorted scraps for bat

- Gray solid fabric: scrap for bat's face

- White fabric: scraps for "BOO!" letters and bat's teeth

- Brown fabric: ⅛ yard

- Black six-strand embroidery thread for bat features and "BOO!" letters

Cutting

BLACK PRINT

- 1 rectangle 1″ × 4″ for bat teeth sections D2 and D3

WHITE

- 1 rectangle 1″ × 4″ for bat teeth sections D2 and D3

BROWN

- 2 strips 1¼″ × 5⅜″ for sashing

- 1 strip 1¼″ × 11″ for sashing

- 2 strips 1½″ × 11″ for sashing

- 2 strips 1½″ × 13″ for sashing

OTHERS

- Cut all other fabrics as each section is assembled.

INSTRUCTIONS

All seam allowances are ¼˝. When possible, press seams between sections in the direction that best reduces bulk.

Assemble the Block

TALL PUMPKIN

1. Assemble all sections.

2. Join section A to B to C.

MEDIUM PUMPKIN

1. Assemble all sections.

2. Join B to C to D.

3. Join A to BCD.

SMALL BOO PUMPKIN

1. Assemble all sections.

2. Join C to D. Join CD to E to F.

3. Join G to H. Join GH to CDEF.

4. Join A to B. Join AB to CDEFGH.

BAT

1. Assemble sections A, B, C, and E.

2. To make pattern pieces D2 and D3 for section D, sew the black and white 1˝ × 4˝ rectangles along the long edge. Press the seam open.

3. Cut at a 45° angle to create pieces for D2 and D3 as shown.

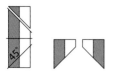

4. Pin fabric for D1 in place on the foundation. Attach D2 using a pin pushed straight through the center seamline on the pattern, ¼˝ in from the diagonal of D2. Stitch the seam, sliding out the pin as you sew. Repeat this step with D3. Assemble the rest of section D.

Line up with seams for D2 and D3.

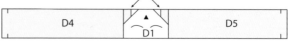

5. Join A to B to C to D to E.

-------------------- TIP --------------------

Using tick marks to assemble blocks is shown in detail at Sew-ichigo.blogspot.com > Tutorials & Tips > Matching Ticks.

6. Trim the blocks to 5⅜˝ × 5⅜˝.

7. Arrange the pumpkin and bat blocks in a 2 × 2 layout. Sew the brown print 1¼˝ × 5⅜˝ strips between the blocks in each row.

8. Sew the rows together, with the brown print 1¼˝ × 11˝ strips between the rows.

9. Sew the brown print 1½˝ × 11˝ strips to the top and bottom of the block. Sew the brown print 1½˝ × 13˝ strips to the sides of the block.

10. Trim the block to 12½″ × 12½″.

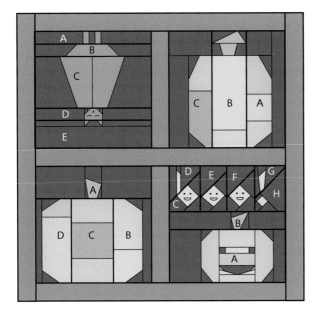

Embroidery

1. Use 2 strands of black embroidery thread to backstitch the mouth and sleeping eyes on the bat. Use satin stitch for the nose.

2. Use 4 strands of black thread to sew French knots for the eyes on the "BOO!" block. Use 2 strands of black thread to backstitch the mouth.

Halloween Boo! Banner

MADE BY Kerry Green • FINISHED BANNER SIZE: 7″ × 2¼ yards

Hanging a banner is an instant way to create seasonal decor and add some cute spooky fun so you're ready for Halloween every year.

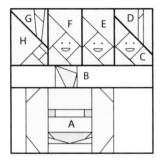
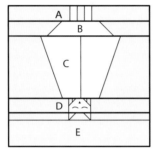
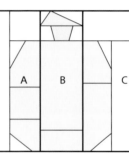
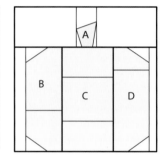

Materials and Supplies

Paper-piecing patterns are on pages CD54–CD57.

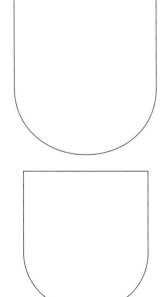

- Orange print fabric: variety to total ¼ yard for pumpkins

- Black print fabric: variety to total ½ yard for background

- Gray print fabric: variety to total ¼ yard for bat's body

- Gray solid fabric: scraps for bat's face

- Green print fabric: scraps for pumpkin stalks

- White fabric: scraps for "BOO!" letters

- Lightweight fusible woven interfacing: ½ yard

- Backing fabric: ¼ yard

- Orange 1″-wide rickrack: 3 yards

- Black 1″-wide cotton twill tape: 2¼ yards

- Water-soluble fabric marker for transferring embroidery markings

- Black six-strand embroidery thread for bat features and "BOO!" letters

- Pinking shears (*optional*)

- Basting/temporary fabric glue, such as Roxanne Glue-Baste-It (*optional*)

OCTOBER—Hide and Seek **83**

BLACK PRINT

- 4 strips 1″ × 5⅜″ for sashing

- 8 strips 1¼″ × 5⅞″ for sashing

- 4 strips 2″ × 6⅞″ for sashing

- 1 strip 1½″ × 5⅜″ for sashing

- 2 strips 1¾″ × 6⅜″ for sashing

- 1 strip 2½″ × 7⅞″ for sashing

- 1 rectangle 1″ × 4″ for bat teeth sections D1 and D2

WHITE

- 1 rectangle 1″ × 4″ for bat teeth sections D1 and D2

BACKING

- 4 using small banner pattern (page CD55)

- 1 using large banner pattern (page CD54)

INTERFACING

- 4 using small banner pattern; trim ¼″ seam allowance from the sides and the lower curved edges (*Do not trim the top edge seam allowance.*)

- 1 using large banner pattern; trim ¼″ seam allowance from the sides and the lower curved edges (*Do not trim the top edge seam allowance.*)

INSTRUCTIONS

All seam allowances are ¼″, unless otherwise stated. Wherever possible, press seams in the direction that best reduces bulk.

Assemble the Block

1. Use the October block instructions (page 80) to make 2 bats, 1 medium pumpkin, 1 tall pumpkin, and 1 "BOO!" pumpkin.

2. To the medium pumpkin, tall pumpkin, and 2 bat blocks:

- Sew black print 1″ × 5⅜″ strip to the top.

- Sew black print 1¼″ × 5⅞″ strips to the sides.

- Sew black print 2″ × 6⅞″ strip to the bottom.

3. To the "BOO!" pumpkin block:

- Sew the black print 1½″ × 5⅜″ strip to the top.

- Sew the black print 1¾″ × 6⅜″ strips to the sides.

- Sew the black print 2½″ × 7⅞″ strip to the bottom.

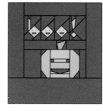

4. Place the large banner pattern on the "BOO!" pumpkin block, pin or trace around it, and cut out. Use the small banner pattern to cut shapes for the other 4 flags.

5. Remove the foundations. Line up the top edges of the flags with the interfacing; then apply the interfacing. The ¼˝ seam allowance will extend beyond the interfacing on the side and bottom edges of each flag.

6. Add embroidery details using the October block instructions (page 81).

Assemble the Banner

1. Place each flag and backing fabric piece right sides together. Leaving the top open, sew the sides and bottom curve with a short stitch. Either trim the seam to ⅛˝ using pinking shears or trim and clip the curves. Turn it right side out and press.

2. Pin or use temporary fabric glue to stick the rickrack to the back of each flag so that just the hump section can be seen from the front. Topstitch on the right side of the flag ⅛˝ in from the edge on the sides and bottom curve of the flag.

3. Fold the twill tape in half lengthwise and press. Open it up and press under ¼˝ of tape at both ends.

4. Sandwich the large flag within the fold in the center of the tape. Pin or glue it in place. Pin or glue the bats, followed by the pumpkins, on both sides of the center flag, leaving a 2˝ gap between each flag.

5. Sew along the full length of the twill tape to secure the flags in place within the fold.

The Snow Bunny

PIECED BY Sonja Callaghan • FINISHED SIZE of paper-pieced block: 12″ × 12″

November finds the ski hills full of snowboarders like Snow Bunny. Her favorite pastime is shredding it up indie style and catching some serious air. This double-cork 1260 block is designed for hardcore paper piecers who've shredded their own fair share of patterns.

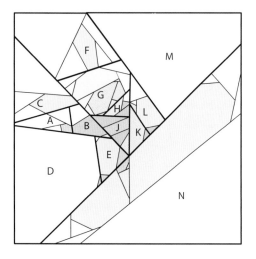

Materials and Supplies

Paper-piecing patterns are on pages CD58–CD61.

- **White solid fabric:** 1 fat quarter for background

- **Assorted solid or near-solid scraps:** total ⅛ yard for ears, helmet, goggles, face, jacket with stripe, pants, gloves, and boots

- **Red solid fabric:** 1 fat eighth for snowboard

- **Contrasting embroidery floss:** for words and flower

INSTRUCTIONS

All seam allowances are ¼˝.

Assemble the Block

1. Assemble each section.

2. Join A to B. Join AB to C. Join D to E. Join ABC to DE.

3. Join F to G to H to J. Join K to L. Join FGHJ to KL.

4. Join ABCDE to FGHJKL to M.

5. Join ABCDEFGHJKLM to N.

6. Trim to 12½˝ × 12½˝

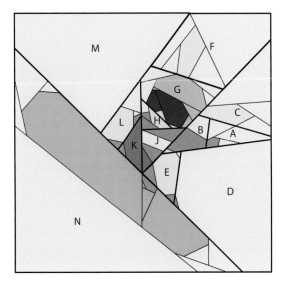

Embroidery

1. Backstitch the words with 6 strands of embroidery floss.

2. Backstitch the flower outline and inner petal lines with 2 strands of embroidery floss.

3. Add French knots to the ends of the flower stamen with 2 strands of embroidery floss.

Snowboarding Bunny Toy

MADE BY Sonja Callaghan • FINISHED TOY SIZE: 12″ × 9″ × 4″

The snowboarding bunny is just too cute to reside solely in a quilt. She wanted to hit the slopes for real! The snow bunny toy makes a perfect gift for children and winter sport fanatics alike!

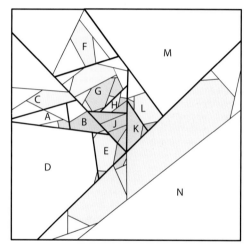

Materials and Supplies

Paper-piecing patterns are on page CD62–CD68.

- **White solid fabric:** ½ yard for background, lining, and backing

- **Assorted scraps:** totaling ⅛ yard for ears, helmet, goggles, face, dark jacket, medium jacket, light jacket stripe, pants, gloves, and boots

- **Polka dot fabric:** ⅛ yard for snowboard

- **4 ounces polyester fiberfill stuffing**

NOTE This toy features fabric from A Stitch in Color by Malka Dubrawsky for Moda.

INSTRUCTIONS

Assemble the Toy

1. Assemble the snow bunny following the November block instructions (page 87). Trim to 12½˝ × 12½˝. Embroider if desired.

2. Use the patterns on pages CD66–CD68 to cut 2 pieces for the lining and backing from the white solid fabric.

3. Cut out the center of the paper pattern at the dotted line. Center the pattern over the Snow Bunny block so that the edge of the pattern is about 1˝ away from the bunny's ears and snowboard. Trace around the pattern and cut out.

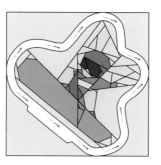

4. Remove the foundation. Layer the lining, snow bunny (right side up), and backing (right side down). Baste.

5. Use a ¼˝ seam allowance to stitch from the left side of the bottom tab all the way around the bunny to the right side, leaving a 4½˝ opening.

6. Press the seam allowances open where the stitching line would be along the tabbed opening.

7. Clip the inner curves and notch the outer curves. Turn right side out and use a point turner to press out all the curves. Press lightly.

8. Stuff so the center of the snow bunny is the fullest, tapering down toward the curved corners.

9. Pin the opening closed and ladder stitch shut.

Little House in the Woods

PIECED BY Kerry Green • **FINISHED SIZE of paper-pieced block: 12˝ × 12˝**

A little light glowing in the midst of the winter darkness—home is where we all want to be in December.

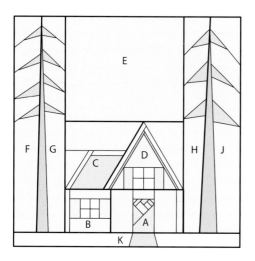

Materials and Supplies

Paper-piecing patterns are on pages CD69–CD72.

- Red fabric: scraps for heart
- Brown fabric: scraps for door
- Yellow fabric: scraps totaling ⅛ yard for house
- Light-colored Christmas or winter print fabric: scraps for windows
- Red print fabric: scraps for window shutters
- Light brown fabric: scrap for house framing
- Gray fabric: 1 fat eighth for roof
- White fabric: 1 fat eighth for roof and snowy ground
- Navy fabric: 1 fat quarter for background

- Green print fabrics: scraps to equal 1 fat eighth for trees and path
- Dark brown fabric: 3″ × 12″ for tree trunks
- Cotton twill tape, ½″ wide: 1 yard for letters
- Stamps and ink pad (such as VersaCraft) or fine permanent pen (such as Pigma Micron) for letters
- Contrasting thread for embroidery
- Water-soluble marker
- French curve ruler *(optional)*
- Pinking shears *(optional)*

Cutting

LIGHT-COLORED CHRISTMAS/WINTER PRINT

- 8 squares 1¼″ × 1¼″ for windows B1 and D1

DARK BROWN

- 2 strips 1½″ × 12″ for tree trunks

COTTON TAPE

- 1″ strips (Cut 1 for each letter in the greeting of your choice.)

---------------------- **TIP** ----------------------

Pinking shears can be used to add a decorative edge for the cotton tape and to prevent fraying.

INSTRUCTIONS

All seam allowances are ¼˝.

Assemble the Block

1. Assemble section A.

2. Section B: Sew the Christmas/winter fabric 1¼˝ × 1¼˝ squares into a four-patch. Trim to 1½˝ square and place the center of the four-patch exactly where the seams meet.

3. Line up the center point of the square with the center of B1 and pin in place.

-------------------- **TIP** --------------------

Push a pin through the center point, perpendicular to the square and foundation, to align the pieces. Use additional pins to secure in place.

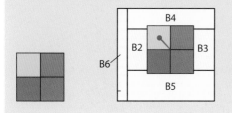

----

4. Assemble the rest of section B.

5. Assemble sections C and D. Use the same technique as you used for B1 to make D1 (see Step 2), but trim the square to 1¾˝ × 1¾˝.

6. Join A to B and C to D. Join AB to CD. Join E to ABCD.

7. Assemble sections F, G, H, and J. Use the brown 1½˝ × 12˝ strips for G10 and J8. Join F to G and join H to J.

8. Attach FG to the BC side of the house. Attach HJ to the AD side of the house.

9. For each letter in your greeting, fold ¼˝ over at one short edge on each piece of cotton tape; press.

10. Stamp a letter below the ¼˝ fold on each strip. Fix the ink with an iron. (Or use a fine permanent fabric marker pen to write the letters.)

11. Mark the center point between the trees by pressing a light fold in the fabric. Use plates or a French curve ruler or draw freehand 2 curved lines with a water-soluble marker, with the first curve beginning and ending at the top of the trees and the second starting an inch below the first and dropping down lower in the center.

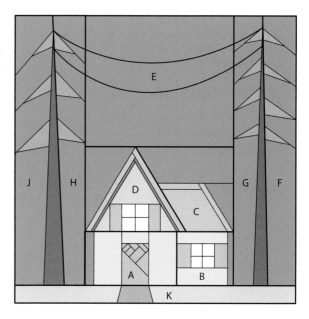

12. Starting with the center letter of the upper curve, pin the letters upside down so the letter side lies against the fabric and the fold in the strip is along the curve. Using light-colored thread, machine stitch along the curve and through the folds in each strip. Flip the letters down to cover the stitching line; hand stitch the sides of the tape in place.

13. Repeat Step 12 for the lower curve to sew the remaining letters in the greeting.

Winter Present Basket

MADE BY Kerry Green • FINISHED BOX SIZE: approximately 12″ × 12″ × 12″

This basket has a hook-and-loop tape binding around the top edge so that cardboard inserts can be removed for storage with your seasonal decorations.

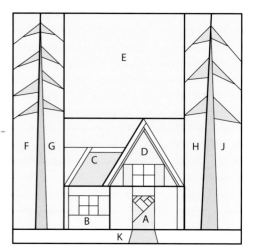

Materials and Supplies

Paper-piecing patterns are on pages CD73–CD76.

- **Red fabric:** scraps for heart

- **Brown fabric:** scraps for door

- **Yellow fabric:** scraps totaling ⅛ yard for house

- **Light-colored Christmas or winter print fabric:** scraps for windows

- **Red print fabric:** scraps for window shutters

- **Light brown fabric:** scrap for house framing

- **Gray fabric:** 1 fat eighth for roof

- **White fabric:** 1 fat eighth for roof and snowy ground

- **Navy fabric:** 1½ yards for background and binding

- **Green print fabrics:** scraps to equal ¼ yard for trees and path

- **Dark brown fabric:** ⅛ yard for tree trunks

- **Cotton twill tape, ½″ wide:** ¾ yard for letters

- **Lining fabric:** ⅞ yard quilting cotton or 5 squares each measuring 12½″ × 12½″

- **Heavyweight fusible fleece (such as Vilene H640 or Pellon TP971F):** 1 yard

- **Lightweight woven fusible interfacing:** 1 yard, at least 24″ wide

- **White hook-and-loop tape:** 1½ yards

- **Stiff cardboard (from packaging boxes, for example):** 4 squares 11⅝″ × 11⅝″ for basket sides

- **Stamps and ink pad** (such as VersaCraft) **or fine permanent pen** (such as Pigma Micron) for letters

- **Contrasting embroidery thread**

- **French curve ruler** (*optional*)

- **Pinking shears** (*optional*)

Cutting

WHITE/WINTER

- 8 squares 1¼″ × 1¼″ for windows B1 and D1

- 3 strips 1¼″ × 12½″ for forest blocks and back of basket

DARK BROWN

- 6 strips 1½″ × 12″ for tree trunks

- 1 strip 2½″ × 12½″ for handles

NAVY

- 1 square 12½″ × 12½″ for base of basket

- 1 rectangle 11¾″ × 12½″ for back of basket

- 2 strips 2″ × 11¾″ for forest blocks

- 2 strips 3½″ × 11¾″ for forest blocks

- 2 strips 2¼″ × 11¾″ for forest blocks

- 2 squares 3½″ × 3½″ for forest blocks

- 2 strips 4″ × width of fabric strips; join and trim to make a continuous strip 4″ × 60″ for binding

LINING

- 5 squares 12½″ × 12½″ for basket lining

HEAVYWEIGHT FUSIBLE FLEECE

- 5 squares 12″ × 12″ for basket

LIGHTWEIGHT WOVEN INTERFACING

- 5 squares 12″ × 12″ for lining

- 1 rectangle 2″ × 12½″ for handles

COTTON TAPE

- ½″ × 1″ strips (Cut 1 for each letter in the greeting of your choice.)

HOOK-AND-LOOP TAPE

- 4 strips 11½″ long

INSTRUCTIONS

All seam allowances are ¼″. Where possible, press seams in the direction that best reduces bulk. The blocks are foundation pieced.

Assemble the Block

1. Follow the December block instructions (page 94) to make the house block, but without the curved lines and the greeting (the greeting will be added in Step 9).

2. Print 2 sets of foundations for sections F, G, H, and J. Make 2 trees using F and G and 2 trees using H and J.

3. For 1 FG tree, trim 3″ from the bottom of the tree trunk. Sew a navy 3¼″ × 3½″ strip to the top of the tree.

4. For 1 HJ tree, trim 3″ from the bottom of the tree trunk. Sew a navy 3½″ square to the top of the tree.

5. Make 2 forest blocks. Sew a navy 3½″ × 11¾″ strip between the full-size FG tree and the small HJ tree. Sew a navy 2″ × 11¾″ strip to one side of the trees and a navy 2¼″ × 11¾″ strip to the other side.

6. Repeat Step 5 for the full-size HJ tree and the small FG tree to make a total of 2 forest blocks.

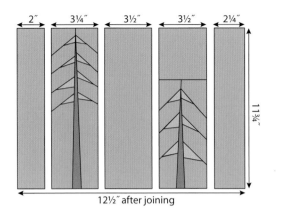

2″ 3¼″ 3½″ 3½″ 2¼″

11¾″

12½″ after joining

7. For the back and sides of the basket, sew a white 1¼″ × 12½″ strip to the bottom of each forest block and to the navy 11¾″ × 12½″ rectangle.

8. Remove the foundations from all of the pieced blocks. Iron the fusible fleece to the back of the house block, the 2 forest blocks, the navy block for the back, and the navy 12½″ square for the base. There should be a ¼″ seam allowance around the edges of the fleece.

9. Stitch the greeting to the house block following Steps 9–13 for the December block (pages 94 and 95).

10. On the reverse side of the forest, house, and background blocks, mark ¼″ in from each corner with pencil. Repeat for all the corners of the base fabric square.

11. Iron the lightweight interfacing to the back of the lining squares. There should be a ¼″ seam allowance around all the edges of the interfacing. Mark ¼″ in from each corner of the squares.

12. Center and apply the interfacing to the wrong side of the handle strip. Fold the strip lengthwise, right sides together, and stitch a ¼″ seam. Turn and press so the seamline runs

down the center of the back of the handle. Topstitch as shown.

13. Cut the handle strip into 2 equal lengths. Turn under and press ½″ at the short ends of each handle. Position the handles on the outer basket, 2½″ from the top edge and 3½″ in from the side seam. Stitch a ½″-wide "X" shape through the handle and basket to reinforce both ends of the handle.

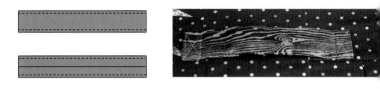

14. Arrange the squares in a plus (+) shape around the base square.

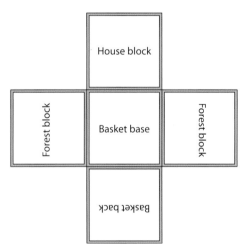

15. Stitch the bottom edge of the squares to the base square, starting and ending each seam precisely at the corner pencil marks. Press the seams open.

16. Join the side edges of each square to make a basket shape. Start each seam at the pencil marks at the bottom corners and stitch to the end of the seam. Turn right side out.

17. Repeat Steps 14–16 for the lining, but leave the lining basket inside out.

18. Press under a ⅜″ hem around the top edge of the lining and stitch ¼″ from the edge. Pin the hooked part of the hook-and-loop tape strips to the top edge on the right side of the lining and stitch around the edge of each strip. To avoid bulk, start placing the hook-and-loop tape strips ¼″ from each corner.

19. Fold the binding strip in half lengthwise, wrong sides together, and press. Bind the top edge of the basket exterior, starting and ending at the back of the basket. Zigzag or serge the seam to finish it; then press it downward. Press the binding at the basket corners to create a vertical crease.

20. Sew the loop part of the hook-and-loop tape strips to the inside of the binding. Use the corner creases to align the strips with the matching hook part of the hook-and-loop tape strips.

21. Place the lining inside the basket exterior, wrong sides together, keeping the hook-and-loop tape open and the binding up. Line up the side seams; then pin and baste. Stitch through the side seams as far down as possible to form pockets for the cardboard inserts.

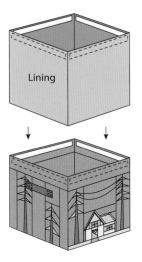

22. Fold the binding back so the pockets are open. Slide in the cardboard. Fold the binding over the top and fasten with hook-and-loop tape.

Section Two:
SMALL PROJECTS
FOR AROUND THE HOUSE

Grapefruit Coasters

MADE BY Ayumi Takahashi • FINISHED SIZE of each wedge: 5″ × 5″

Looking for quick and fun last-minute gifts? How about these grapefruit coasters? Use up your favorite fabric scraps in yellow shades (or other fruity colors) and turn them into a set of four coasters.

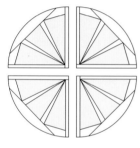

Materials and Supplies

Makes 4 coasters.
Paper-piecing patterns are on page CD77.

- White solid fabric: ½ yard for front and back

- Assorted print scraps: 12 pieces at least 2¾″ × 5″

- Yellow solid fabric: ⅛ yard for binding

- Batting: 4 pieces 6″ × 6″

- Quilt adhesive spray

- Point turner

Cutting

WHITE SOLID

- 4 quarter-circles using the coaster pattern

YELLOW SOLID

- 4 strips 1⅝″ × 8½″ on the bias for binding

INSTRUCTIONS

Assemble the Coaster

1. Print 4 copies of the coaster foundation.

2. Arrange the 12 print scraps in a circle. Assemble a coaster using the white solid and 3 scraps. Press.

3. Trim ¼″ from the straight edges and ⅜″ from the curved edge. Remove the foundation. Use quilt adhesive spray to attach it to the batting.

4. Quilt parallel lines about ⅜″ apart. Trim excess batting.

NOTE Quilt each coaster so the quilting lines are parallel when the coasters are placed in a circle.

5. Place a white quarter-circle on top of the quilted piece, right sides together. Using a ¼″ seam allowance, sew along the 2 straight edges. Trim the seam allowance to ⅛″ to reduce bulk.

6. Turn right side out and use a point turner to push out the corner. Press. Pin the curved edge so the layers meet. Baste.

7. Pin a yellow binding strip along the curved edge so it hangs over both ends. Sew on the binding using a ⅜″ seam allowance.

8. Fold the overhanging ends of the binding to the back of the coaster. Hand stitch the binding to the back, tucking under the ends at both sides.

9. Repeat Steps 2–8 to make 4 coasters.

Liberty Street

POTHOLDER

FINISHED BLOCK SIZE: 9″ × 9″ • **FINISHED POTHOLDER SIZE: 8½″ diameter**

MADE BY Kylie Seldon

Inspired by the streets of San Francisco, this potholder makes a pretty place to rest your teapot, or even a lovely little wallhanging. The streets are pieced using the Liberty Lifestyle Bloomsbury Gardens line, paired with natural linen to let the gorgeous, saturated colors shine. The binding fabric is Heath in Chocolate by Alexander Henry.

Materials and Supplies

Paper-piecing patterns are on pages CD78–CD80.

- **6 assorted print fabrics:** scraps for piecing the shops

- **Natural linen fabric:** 1 fat quarter for piecing the background

- **Backing fabric:** 10″ × 10″

- **Binding fabric:** 12″ × 12″

- **Cotton batting:** 10″ × 10″ for interlining

- **Thermal batting** (I used Insul-Bright by The Warm Company.): 10″ × 10″

- **Cotton lace trim, ribbon, or tape:** 5½″ for hanging loop

- **Fine black permanent marker** (such as Artline 200 0.4)

- **Small alphabet stamp set** for shop signs (Each letter in my set is about ¼″ tall.)

- **Fabric ink stamp pad** (I used VersaCraft ink in Espresso.) and **stamps** to fit shop windows

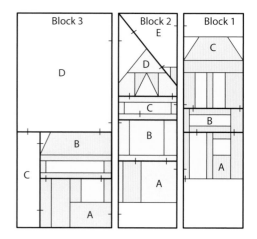

DESIGN NOTE This block would look great in a scrappy collection of prints from your stash with fussy-cut images and text, instead of the stamped linen. Japanese novelty prints are a fantastic source of cute fussy cuts for piecing into windows.

Cutting

BINDING

- Cut the 12″ × 12″ square on the diagonal. Cut 3 bias strips 2″ wide for single-fold bias binding.

The potholder's fabric labels read:

cafe

fabric

COTTON
embroidery thread

patisserie

INSTRUCTIONS

All seam allowances are ¼˝.

Read all instructions before starting to piece your block.

Assemble the Block

1. Assemble each section in each shop block.

------------------------------ TIP ------------------------------

Assemble one shop block at a time to avoid confusion. Refer to the project photo (page 105) and block illustrations to help with fabric placement. Use the linen background fabric for the shop windows and signs.

----

2. For shop block 1, join A to B to C.

3. For shop block 2, join E to D. Join A to B to C to ED.

4. For shop block 3, join A to B to C to D.

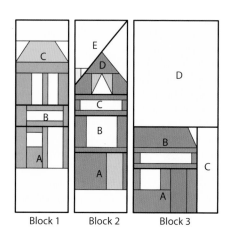

Block 1   Block 2   Block 3

------------------------------ TIP ------------------------------

To sew two sections together, line up the corresponding tick marks and pin straight through. Keeping these initial pins completely straight and vertical as possible, add more pins on each side before sewing.

Increase your machine's stitch length to 3mm and sew along the seamline to baste. Check to make sure the sections are well aligned before sewing back over the seam with a shorter stitch length.

----

5. Sew the 3 blocks together and trim to 9˝ × 9˝.

6. Using the illustration as a guide, trim the bottom left corner from the block by cutting ¼˝ below where the stitching line will be to allow for the seam allowance.

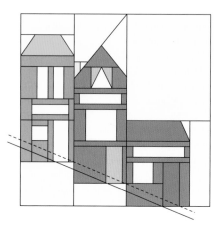

7. Trace around the triangle you just trimmed on the linen background fabric. Add ½˝ on all sides and cut out.

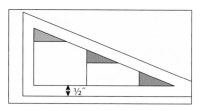

½˝

8. Sew the linen triangle to the pieced block along the diagonal. Press the seam toward the linen and trim the block back to 9˝ × 9˝.

Stamp the Text

Stamp text onto the shop signs. Be creative! What shops will your street have—a grocer, a florist, a pet shop? Stamp coordinating images into the shop windows. Use a hot, dry iron to set the ink.

------------------ **TIP** ------------------

A great tutorial for stamping on fabric can be found at limeriot.blogspot.com > Tutorials > Stamping on Fabric.

------------------ **TIP** ------------------

If stamping directly on your finished block makes you nervous, stamp the text and images onto linen background fabric before piecing the block. Keep in mind the place-ment of any fussy-cut images when piecing.

Assemble and Quilt the Potholder

1. Remove the foundation on the pieced block. Layer the backing fabric square (wrong side up), the cotton batting square, the Insul-Bright square (shiny side up), and the patchwork block (right side up and centered). Baste the layers.

2. Machine or hand quilt as desired. I used dense quilting for the linen background to add texture and make the shops stand out.

Finish and Bind the Potholder

1. Center the circle pattern on the quilted patchwork square and pin in place, or trace around the circle with a fabric pencil. Cut to make an 8½″ diameter circle. Zigzag stitch all around the edge to hold the layers together before applying the binding.

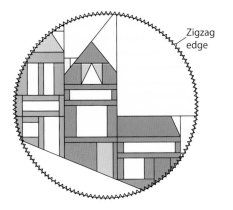

Zigzag edge

2. Fold the 5½″ piece of trim or tape in half to create a loop. Center the loop on the top back edge of the potholder and pin it in place so the loop faces the center of the potholder. Baste in place.

3. Sew the 2″-wide bias strips together to make at least 30″ of single-fold bias binding. Use this to bind the potholder.

4. Fold the hanging loop up and hand sew in place.

Tea Towel

MADE BY Megan Dye • **FINISHED SIZE: 18″ × 24″**

No day is complete without a nice cup of tea. The cup and saucer, sugar bowl, and creamer motifs on this tea towel are just perfect for fussy cutting some of your favorite prints. And, of course, at the end, you have a handy tea towel to wash up your own cup and saucer.

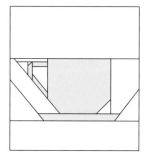  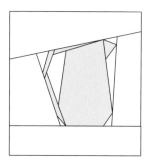

Materials and Supplies

Paper-piecing patterns are on pages CD81–CD83.

- **Scraps:** totaling ¼ yard for motifs
- **White solid:** fat quarter for background of motif blocks
- **Linen:** 19″ × 25″
- **Print fabric:** ¼ yard for ruffle
- **Twill tape:** 1 piece 7½″ long (I used 1″-wide decorative twill tape.)

Cutting

WHITE

- 2 strips 2¼″ × 6″ to sash the blocks

PRINT

- 1 strip 2½″ × width of fabric for ruffle, with selvages trimmed
- 2 strips 2″ × 19″ for ruffle header

INSTRUCTIONS

All seam allowances are ¼˝.

Assemble the Block

1. Assemble 3 tea motif blocks: teacup and saucer, sugar, and creamer.

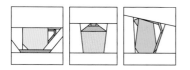

2. Sew the blocks together. Sew a white 2¼˝ × 6˝ strip to each side to make a 20˝ × 6˝ panel.

Make the Ruffle

1. Sew a double-fold hem along both short sides and one long side of the print 2½˝ × width of fabric strip.

2. Baste the unfinished long side and gather into an 18˝-long ruffle.

3. Fold each print 2˝ × 19˝ strip in half lengthwise, wrong sides together, and press. Open and press each raw edge to the center crease. These strips will form the ruffle header.

4. Unfold one of the edges on each header strip. Make a sandwich with one of the strips, the raw edge of the ruffle, and then the other strip as shown. Sew with a ½˝ seam allowance.

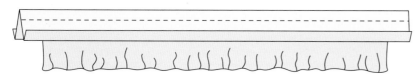

5. Press the header away from the ruffle and topstitch across the header near the ruffle.

Assemble the Tea Towel

1. Measure 9½˝ from the bottom of the linen. Place the pieced tea motif panel upside down, with the top edge of the panel at the 9½˝ mark, right sides together. Stitch along the raw edge using a ¼˝ seam. Remove all the foundations. Fold the panel down toward the bottom of the towel and press.

2. Turn under the bottom edge of the motif panel and press. Topstitch across the top and bottom of the motif panel.

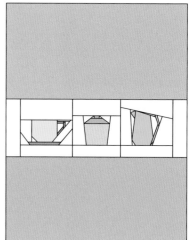

3. Press under ¼˝ around the side and top edges of the linen, leaving the bottom edge raw.

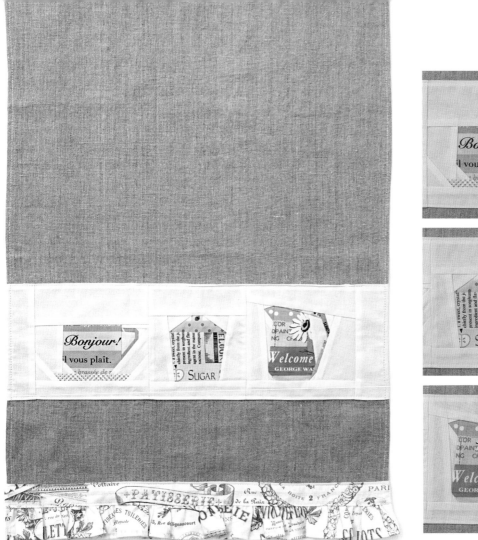

4. Place the 7½″ piece of twill tape diagonally across a top corner on the back of the linen for a hanging loop. Pin or baste in place.

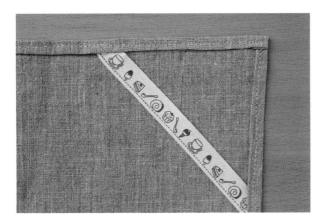

5. Press under another ¼″ around the side and top edges to complete the hem. Sew around the linen, catching the twill tape in the stitching.

6. Center the towel's bottom raw edge inside the ruffle header. The header will be slightly wider than the linen. Sew along the top of the ruffle header, making sure to catch the back in the stitching.

7. Tuck the raw edges of the header toward the back of the towel and hand stitch in place to finish.

Kite Tote

MADE BY Charise Randell

This fun tote has a whimsical paper-pieced kite as its focal point and is framed by colorful borders in a Log Cabin design. It is the perfect size for shopping trips or to hold your crafts on the go!

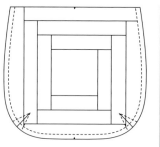

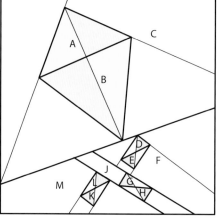

Materials and Supplies

Paper-piecing patterns are on pages CD84–CD88.

- **Blue polka dot fabric:** 1 fat quarter for background of both kites

- **Scraps from 4 different fabrics:** totaling ⅛ yard for both kites

- **Red solid fabric:** 6 scraps 1″ × 1″ for tails on kite 2

- **Pink print fabrics:** 2″-wide scraps totaling ⅛ yard

- **Yellow print fabrics:** 2″-wide scraps totaling ⅛ yard

- **Blue print fabric:** 3″-wide scraps totaling ¼ yard

- **Red gingham fabric:** ⅓ yard for binding and tabs

- **Muslin fabric:** ½ yard for backing

- **Lining fabric:** ½ yard

- **Coordinating fabric:** 10¼″ × 12½″ for pocket

- **Lightweight interfacing:** ⅛ yard

- **Batting:** ½ yard

- **Perle cotton:** red #8 and pink #8 for embroidery

- **1 pair of wood handles:** 8½″ wide × 5″ tall

---- **TIP** ----

You can purchase wooden handles from your local arts and crafts store or from Quilting-Warehouse.com.

Cutting

LINING

• 2 pieces using tote bag pattern

MUSLIN

• 2 squares 16½˝ × 16½˝ for backing

BATTING

• 2 squares 16½˝ × 16½˝

RED GINGHAM

• 2 strips 1⅞˝ × 16˝ on the bias for top edge binding

• 4 strips 3½˝ × 4½˝ for handle tabs

NOTE The measurements given for the handle tabs will work with ⅞˝ openings. Check the openings in your handles and adjust as needed to 4 × the slot width. For example, if the slot opening in the handle is ¾˝, make the tab strip width 4 × ¾˝ = 3˝.

LIGHTWEIGHT INTERFACING

• 4 strips 3½˝ × 4½˝ for handle tabs

INSTRUCTIONS

All seam allowances are ¼˝, unless otherwise noted.

Assemble the Block

1. Assemble section A. Assemble section B. Join A to B.

2. Position AB (just sewn) onto section C (paper foundation). Align seams and pin. Add pieces C1–C4 individually.

3. Assemble section D. Assemble section E. Join D to E.

4. Position DE (sewn) onto section F (paper foundation). Align seams and pin. Add pieces F1–F4 individually.

5. Repeat the technique described in Steps 3–4 to assemble 2 more kite tails: GH with J, and KL with M.

6. Join DEF to GHJ to KLM. Join ABC to DEFGHJKLM.

7. Trim to 5½˝ square.

8. Embroider the kite strings on each block using a backstitch.

9. Repeat Steps 1–8 to make another kite block.

Assemble the Outer Bag

1. Add strips around each kite block Log Cabin style, first adding 2˝ pink strips, followed by 2˝ yellow strips, and finally the 3˝ blue strips.

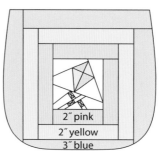

2. Remove the foundations for both kite blocks.

3. Layer a muslin square, batting square, and one of the kite blocks. Baste in place.

4. Stitch in the ditch around the kite block. Stitch ¼″ from the original stitching and continue around the entire block in a spiral pattern.

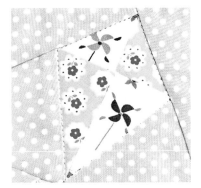

5. Align the top center of the tote bag pattern with the top center of the block. Trace around the pattern and cut out. Mark the darts and notches.

6. Repeat Steps 3–5 for the other kite block.

7. Stitch the darts on both tote bag panels. On one panel, press the darts toward the center. On the other panel, press the darts toward the side seams.

8. Place the tote bag panels right sides together. Position the darts in opposite directions on either side of the bag. Stitch around the perimeter with a ½″ seam allowance. Press the seam open.

Assemble the Lining

1. Fold the 10¼″ × 12½″ piece of fabric for the pocket in half along the 10¼″ side so that the right sides are together. The folded edge will become the top of the pocket.

2. Stitch with a ¼″ seam allowance along the unfolded edges, leaving a 4″ opening at the bottom. Press the seam open. Turn right side out and press.

3. Center the pocket on one of the lining pieces 3½″ from the top edge. Edgestitch around the pocket sides and bottom. Mark and stitch a vertical line 4″ from the edge of the pocket to create 2 pockets.

4. Stitch the darts in both lining pieces. On one piece, press the darts toward the center. On the other piece, press the darts toward the side seams.

5. Place the lining pieces right sides together, positioning the darts in opposite directions on each piece. Stitch around the perimeter with a ½″ seam allowance. Press the seam open.

6. Place the lining, wrong side out, inside the tote bag as shown. Align the top edges and side seams and pin. Baste around the top edge ⅜″ from the raw edge.

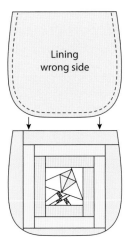

Lining
wrong side

Attach the Handles

1. Apply the interfacing to the wrong side of each handle tab strip.

2. Fold a tab strip in half lengthwise along the 4½˝ edge, wrong sides together, and press. Open and fold the edges to the center crease and press. Topstitch on both long edges. Repeat this step for the additional 3 tabs.

3. Measure the distance between the inside of the handle slot openings. Mark this measurement centered on the top of the tote bag on both sides.

4. Slip the tabs through the handle openings. Baste the raw edges together.

5. Position the tabs on the inside lining, using the markings from Step 3. Baste the raw edges of the handle tabs to the top edge of the tote bag and lining.

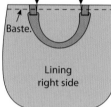

Distance between slots in handle

Baste.

Lining right side

Finish the Bag

1. Cut a 45° angle on the end of each bias tape strip and sew together into a continuous strip. Press the seam open.

2. Make the bias binding by folding the bias strip in half lengthwise and folding the edges in to the center crease, or use a bias tape maker. Open one long folded edge.

3. Fold a short edge of the bias binding under to the wrong side by ⅜˝. Place the folded edge of the bias binding on a side seam of the inside bag, with the right side of the binding facing the right side of the lining.

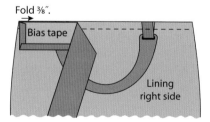

Fold ⅜˝.

Bias tape

Lining right side

4. Matching raw edges, stitch the binding to the lining edge with a ⅜˝ seam allowance. When you reach the starting point, overlap the folded starting point by ½˝.

5. Fold the bias binding to the right side of the tote bag and slipstitch in place to cover the stitching.

Nutcracker Pillow

MADE BY Chase Wu • FINISHED PILLOW SIZE: 14½″ × 14½″

This classic holiday pillow is made with retro prints and embellished with an embroidered mustache that brings texture to the pillow and makes the soldier come to life. He stands ready for his next dance! Bring on the sugar plum fairies!

Material and Supplies

Paper-piecing patterns are on page CD89.

- **Assorted print fabrics:** scraps totaling ⅓ yard (I used 10 pieces 5″ × 9″ to piece the ribbon and the nutcracker.)

- **Background fabric:** 1 fat quarter

- **Backing fabric:** ½ yard

- **Cotton batting:** 16″ × 16″

- **Unbleached muslin:** 16″ × 16″

- **Embroidery floss:** 1 skein DMC 3772

- **Spray adhesive,** such as Elmer's Craft Bond

- **Water-soluble pen**

- **14″ pillow form**

Cutting

BACKGROUND

- 2 strips 4⅞″ × 11″ for sides

- 1 strip 2½″ × 11″ between ribbon and nutcracker

- 2 strips 2½″ × 15″ for top and bottom

BACKING

- 1 piece 12″ × 15″

- 1 piece 8″ × 15″

INSTRUCTIONS

All seam allowances are ¼˝.

Assemble the Nutcracker and Ribbon

1. Assemble all sections for the nutcracker and ribbon.

2. Join B to C. Join D to E to F. Join G to H. Join J to K. Join GH to JK.

3. Join BC to DEF to GHJK.

4. Trim nutcracker to 3⅜˝ × 11˝. Trim ribbon to 1½˝ × 11˝

Assemble the Pillow Front

1. Sew the background 2½˝ × 11˝ strip between the ribbon and the nutcracker. Sew a background 4⅞˝ × 11˝ strip to the left and another strip to the right. Press the seams open.

2. Use a fine point water-soluble pen (I like Mark-B-Gone by Dritz.) to trace the mustache onto the nutcracker's face. Using 2 embroidery floss strands, outline the mustache contour. Remove the paper foundation. Using 6 embroidery floss strands, fill in the mustache with satin stitch.

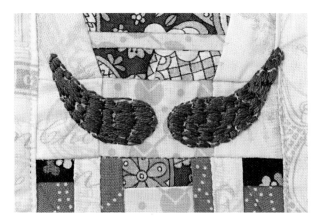

3. Sew the background 2½˝ × 15˝ strips to the top and bottom of the block. Press the seams open. Trim the pillow top to 15˝ × 15˝.

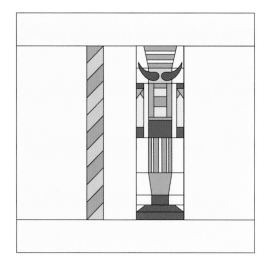

4. Layer the pillow front, batting, and muslin. Baste and quilt.

Assemble the Envelope Back

1. Sew a ¼˝ double hem along a long edge of each backing piece. Topstitch along the hem's inner and outer edge.

2. Position the backing pieces so they overlap on top of the pillow front, right sides facing. Sew around the pillow's perimeter.

3. Trim away excess fabric and batting. Zigzag stitch around the pillow's perimeter or use a serger to finish the inside seams. Trim the corners and turn right side out.

Mail Organizer

FINISHED BASKET SIZE: 9″ × 2″ × 8″ long • **FINISHED ORGANIZER SIZE: 9″ × 2″ × 31½″, including ribbons**

MADE BY Ayumi Takahashi

This letter organizer showcases three paper-pieced designs that tell a story about a letter's delivery. It is exciting to think about a letter's journey, especially when you know the letter was written just for you by someone special.

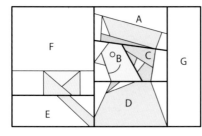 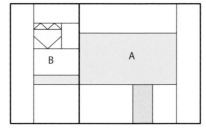 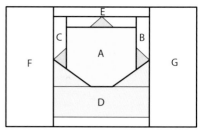

Materials and Supplies

Paper-piecing patterns are on pages CD90–CD94.

- **Green solid fabric:** 1 fat eighth for back of top pocket

- **Beige solid fabric:** 1 fat eighth for back of middle pocket

- **Coral solid fabric:** 1 fat eighth for back of bottom pocket

- **Polka dot fabrics:** totaling ¼ yard for 3 pocket bottoms

- **Coordinating fabric:** 3 fat quarters for pocket linings

- **Assorted scraps** for paper piecing

- **Lightweight fusible interfacing:** 1 yard for pockets

- **Heavyweight fusible interfacing:** 1 yard for lining

- **⅝″ linen tape:** 1 yard for ribbons

- **Red six-strand embroidery floss** for mailman's mouth

- **½″ black button:** 1 for mailman's eye

- **½″ buttons:** 10 for back of pockets

- **Water-soluble pen**

- **Letter stamps and ink pad for fabric** (*optional*)

Cutting

GREEN, BEIGE, AND CORAL

- 1 rectangle in each color 6¾″ × 10½
  for pocket backs

POLKA DOT

- 3 rectangles 6½″ × 10½″ for pocket bottoms

COORDINATING FABRIC

- 3 rectangles 10½″ × 19″ for lining pockets

LINEN TAPE

- 1 strip 10″ for top hanging loop

- 4 strips 6″ for middle and bottom ribbons

LIGHTWEIGHT FUSIBLE INTERFACING

- 3 rectangles 9⅞″ × 18⅜″ for 3 pocket exteriors

HEAVYWEIGHT FUSIBLE INTERFACING

- 3 rectangles 9¾″ × 18¼″ for 3 pocket linings

INSTRUCTIONS

Assemble the Mailman Pocket

1. Assemble all sections.

2. Join B to C. Join A to BC to D. Join E to F. Join ABCD to EF to G. Trim the block to 6¾″ × 10½″.

3. Remove the foundation. Embroider the mailman's mouth using a backstitch.

4. Sew a polka dot 6½″ × 10½″ rectangle followed by the green 6¾″ × 10½″ rectangle to the bottom of the mailman block.

5. Center an interfacing 9⅞″ × 18⅜″ piece on the wrong side of the mailman pocket and fuse it in place. Attach the black button for the mailman's eye.

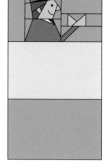

6. Fold the mailman pocket in half, right sides facing, and sew the side edges together.

7. Create box corners at both sides of the bottom of the pocket. Flatten the corners and center the

seam, and draw a 2″ line across the corner. Sew along the line and cut off the excess, leaving a ¼″ seam allowance.

8. Fuse a heavyweight interfacing rectangle to the wrong side of a lining rectangle. Make the lining by following Steps 6 and 7.

9. Turn the basket exterior and lining so the seams are on the outside. To fix the lining in place, match up the box seams of the basket exterior with the box seams of the lining, and pin. Sew once again along the box seams, sewing through both the lining and basket exterior.

10. Turn the pocket right side out. Fold ¼″ under along the top edge of both the lining and the exterior and press to create a crease. Hand stitch the lining and the exterior pocket together.

Assemble the Mailbox Pocket

1. Assemble sections A and B. Join A to B.

2. Trim to 6¾″ × 10½″. Remove the foundation.

3. Follow Steps 4–10 of "Assemble the Mailman Pocket" to complete the mailbox pocket, using the beige solid and polka dot fabrics.

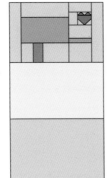

Assemble the Envelope Pocket

1. Stamp a message on a piece of fabric at least ¼″ larger all around than piece A4. Press to set the ink.

------------------ **TIP** ------------------

If you don't have letter stamps, you can substitute with a text print fabric or even a cute fussy-cut design.

----

2. Assemble section A using the stamped fabric for A4. Assemble B and C. Join C to A. Join B to CA.

3. Add pieces D1–D4 individually.

4. Follow Steps 4–10 of "Assemble the Mailman Pocket" to complete the envelope pocket, using the coral solid and polka dot fabrics.

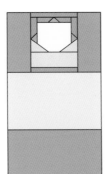

Assemble the Mail Organizer

1. Sew a ⅜″ double-fold hem along both short edges of all the linen tape strips.

2. Using a water-soluble pen, mark 2¾″ in from each side on the top edge of the back of all 3 pockets.

3. Mark 2¾″ in from each side at the top of the polka dot base on the back of the mailman and mailbox pockets.

4. Align the ends of the 10″ strip of tape with the marks on the top edge of the mailman pocket, placing the folded-under edges against the back of the pocket. Sew very close to the top edge to join the tape to the pocket.

5. Align one end of the 6″ strip of tape with one of the marks on the polka dot base seam on the mailman pocket. Sew in place and attach a button on top of the tape to further secure. Repeat for the other mark on the polka dot seam, using a second 6″ strip and button.

6. Repeat Step 5 for the mailbox pocket.

7. Line up the open ends of the 6″ strips on the mailman pocket with the marks on the top of the mailbox pocket and stitch in place.

8. Line up the open ends of the 6″ strips on the mailbox pocket with the marks on the top of the envelope pocket and stitch in place.

Artist's Portfolio

FINISHED BLOCK SIZE: 16″ × 8″   •   **FINISHED SIZE WHEN OPENED: 21″ × 32″**

MADE BY Cheryl Arkison

Children are prolific artists. They churn out drawings as fast as you can say "paper piecing." Keeping every single one would be impossible, but there are always special ones you just can't bear to part with. This artist's portfolio is a place to store the most precious of artwork. Of course, that's only one possible use—an artist will think of many more!

Materials and Supplies

Paper-piecing patterns are on pages CD95–CD99.

- **Assorted color fabrics:** 16 strips 3″ × 12″ for rainbow fan
- **Text fabric:** ¾ yard for background
- **Stripe fabric:** 1¼ yards for backing and binding
- **Batting:** 23″ × 34″
- **Heavyweight interfacing, 20″ wide:** 1 yard
- **Freezer paper**
- **Coordinating thread**

Cutting

TEXT FABRIC

- 16 squares 2½″ × 2½″ to piece the rainbow fan
- 1 rectangle 9″ × 17″; from this rectangle, cut 1 piece using template A and 1 piece using template B
- 2 strips 4½″ × 21″ to sash the rainbow block
- 2 strips 2½″ × 21″ to sash the rainbow block
- 4 strips 2¾″ × 8½″ to sash the rainbow block

STRIPE

- 1 piece 21″ × 32½″ for lining
- 1 strip 3½″ × 21″ for bottom of portfolio
- 6 strips 3″ × width of fabric; join 3 of the strips into 1 continuous strip to use for binding. From the remaining strips, cut:
  – 8 strips 3″ × 7″ for ties
  – 2 strips 3″ × 14″ for handles

INTERFACING

- 2 pieces 14″ × 20″

INSTRUCTIONS

Assemble the Portfolio Cover

1. Make a copy of the rainbow fan on the matte side of freezer paper. Cut out the whole foundation, not the individual pieces.

NOTE This project uses basic foundation piecing with freezer paper as the foundation material. Remember, the finished piece will be the mirror image of the pattern.

2. Arrange the 16 fabric strips in a pleasing pattern.

3. Assemble the rainbow using the color strips and the text fabric 2½˝ squares.

NOTE Keep the large fabric trimmings for the back of the portfolio.

4. Fold the text fabric template A piece in half and finger-press. Open it and fold the sides toward the middle to find the quarter marks. Finger-press and open.

5. Fold the rainbow fan block in half and then in half again. Finger-press to mark the folds.

6. Pin the center fold on the text template B piece to the center of the rainbow, right sides together and between pieces 15 and 17. Pin at the ends and at the remaining fold marks. Add 2–3 more pins between each fold. Make sure there is no puckered fabric between the pins.

7. With the rainbow arc on top, *start sewing from the center pin* around one side. Remove the pins as you sew. To sew the other half of the seam, flip the block over and sew with the text fabric on top, again starting from the center and sewing to the other side. Be careful not to pull the rainbow block as you sew. Press the seam open.

NOTE Sewing this seam in two steps, each time starting in the middle, will help you keep the rainbow fan exactly centered.

8. Repeat Steps 4–7 with the text fabric template B piece and the bottom of the rainbow fan. This time, sew the entire seam with the rainbow circle on top. Clip the seam allowance 4 times and press open.

9. Sew a text fabric 2¾˝ × 8½˝ strip to both sides of the rainbow. Sew a text fabric 4½˝ × 21˝ strip to the top of the block and a 3˝ × 21˝ strip to the bottom.

Assemble the Portfolio Back

1. Cut the leftover scraps from making the rainbow block into 2½˝ × 2½˝ squares. You need a total of 32 squares.

-------------------- **TIP** --------------------

If needed, cut squares from any excess text fabric and add them to the mix.

2. Sew the squares together into an 4 × 8 patchwork section measuring 8½˝ × 16½˝. Press.

3. Sew a text fabric 2¾˝ × 8½˝ strip to both sides of the block. Sew a text fabric 4½˝ × 21˝ strip to the top of the block and a 3˝ × 21˝ strip to the bottom.

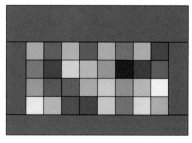

Assemble the Portfolio

1. Sew the stripe 3½″ × 21″ strip between the bottom edges of the portfolio cover and back.

2. Remove the foundation from the rainbow block. Baste the exterior of the portfolio to the batting. Use quilting to add texture and to keep it from slumping once assembled. Trim any excess batting.

3. To prepare the lining, apply the 2 pieces of fusible interfacing to the 21″ × 32½″ stripe fabric. Leave ½″ of fabric around the top and side edges of each piece of interfacing.

4. Fold the handle and tie strips in half lengthwise, right sides together. Sew along the long side for all strips. Sew along a short side for each tie. Turn the strips right side out, using a turning tube or a large safety pin attached to an end.

5. Topstitch ⅛″ from the edges for each tie. Topstitch ⅛″ from the long sides of the 14″ handle.

6. Layer the lining and portfolio wrong sides together. Machine sew the binding to the portfolio.

7. Turn the portfolio over so the lining faces up. Mark the center of one end and then mark 3″ to each side of center. Pin the ends of the 14″ handle strip at these marks, being careful not to twist the strip. Repeat for the other end.

8. Pin the ties 5″ and 10″ from the top and bottom, on both sides.

9. Machine stitch over the handle and ties to attach them, sewing within the seam allowance of the binding.

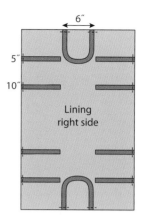

------------------ **TIP** ------------------

If you are machine finishing the binding, you can skip tacking down the ties and handle because you will catch the ties and handles in that stitching.

10. Finish the binding by hand or machine.

Sewing Machine Cover

FINISHED SIZE of paper-pieced block: 11¼″ × 11¼″ • **FINISHED COVER SIZE: 16″ × 31″**

MADE BY Caroline M. Press

Natural linen and modern fabrics combine to make a stylish, practical cover for your sewing machine. This sewing machine cover is designed to fit most sewing machines because it has easy tie closures.

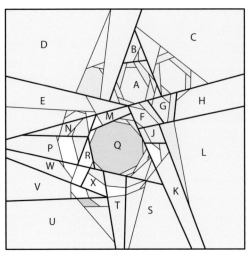

Materials and Supplies

Paper-piecing patterns are on pages CD100–CD103.

- **Linen background fabric:** ¾ yard for the cover and notion block background

- **Red fabric:** scraps for scissors

- **Gold fabric:** small scrap for thimble

- **2 similar color fabrics:** scraps for measuring tape

- **2 similar color fabrics:** scraps for measuring tape dispenser

- **Print fabric:** ⅞ yard for lining, ties, and binding

- **Batting:** 17″ × 32″

- **Gluestick**

- **Water-soluble pen**

- **Embroidery floss**

Cutting

LINEN

- 1 strip 5″ × 12″ for side of block
- 1 piece 16″ × 20″ for cover
- Use the remaining linen to construct the notions block.

PRINT

- 5 strips 2″ × width of fabric for double-fold binding and ties
- 1 rectangle 16″ × 31″ for lining

INSTRUCTIONS

All seam allowances are ¼˝, except where noted.

Assemble the Block

------------------- **TIP** -------------------

If a pin would get in the way of sewing, use a gluestick to hold down tiny pieces of fabric.

----

1. Assemble all sections.

2. Join B to A to C to D to E.

3. Join F to G to H. Join J to K to L. Join JKL to FGH.

4. Join N to P. Join M to Q to R. Join NP to MQR.

5. Join S to T. Join W to X to V to U. Join WXVU to ST.

6. Join WXVUST to NPMQR to FGHJKL to ABCDE.

7. Trim the pieced block to 12˝ × 12˝.

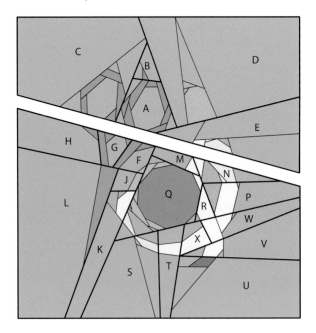

Assemble the Cover

NOTE All seam allowances for cover assembly instructions are ½˝.

Sew the linen 5˝ × 12˝ strip to the right of the block and the linen 16˝ × 20˝ piece to the top. Press.

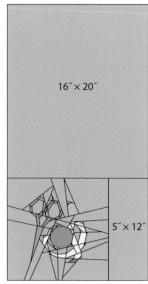

Embroidery

Use the embroidery templates on page CD103 and a water-soluble marker to write "S-E-W" on the linen 5˝ × 12˝ strip. Use a running stitch and 4 strands of black embroidery floss to outline the letters.

Quilt and Finish the Cover

1. Remove the foundation. Layer the print 16˝ × 31˝ lining (right side down), batting, and sewing machine cover (right side up) and baste in place. Quilt by hand or machine.

2. Use a water-soluble marker to mark 7˝ from both corners of the cover along the long sides.

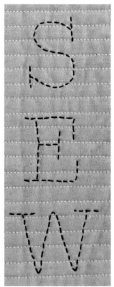

3. Make double-fold tape using the 2 print 2″ × width of fabric strips. Use a bias tape maker. Or press the 2″ strip in half lengthwise, open and bring raw edges to the crease, and fold in half again. Topstitch along the edge to secure. Cut each strip in half to make 4 ties total.

4. Position ties at each 7″ mark along the edge. Baste in place.

5. Bind the cover.

6. Tie a knot in the tie ends to keep them from fraying.

7″   7″

Lining

7″   7″

Coat Hanger
WALL ART

MADE BY Leila Beasley • **FINISHED SIZE: 10˝ × 14˝**

Why not start a collection of embroidery hoop wall art? They look great grouped together in different shapes and sizes! And it is a fun way to display some of your favorite fabrics and paper-pieced blocks.

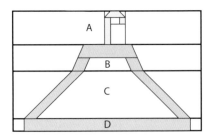

Materials and Supplies

Paper-piecing patterns are on page CD104.

- **Polka dot fabric:** 1 fat quarter for background
- **Wood-grain fabric:** 1 fat eighth for hanger
- **Black fabric:** small scraps for hook
- **Backing fabric:** 1 fat quarter
- **Oval embroidery hoop:** 8˝ × 12˝

Cutting

POLKA DOT

- 2 strips 3¼˝ × 5½˝ to sash the block
- 2 strips 2¾˝ × 14˝ to sash the block

BACKING

- 1 piece 10˝ × 14˝

INSTRUCTIONS

All seam allowances are ¼˝.

Assemble the Block

1. Assemble all sections. Join A to B to C to D. Trim to 5½˝ × 8½˝.

2. Sew the polka dot 3¼˝ × 5½˝ strips to the sides of the block and the polka dot 2¾˝ × 14˝ strips to the top and bottom.

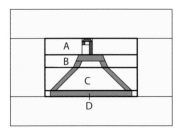

Assemble the Wallhanging

1. Place the finished block on top of the backing fabric.

2. Place both layers on top of the bottom half of the embroidery hoop. Make sure the block is centered.

3. Push the top half of the embroidery hoop down over the block. Smooth out any wrinkles before securing the block inside the embroidery hoop. Trim away excess fabric on the back.

Celebration Pennant

MADE BY Amy Lobsiger • FINISHED SIZE: 12¾˝ × 14˝

This cheerful pennant can be the central focus of any festive decor. It can also set the stage for a celebration of spring. This project features foundation piecing, insert piecing, and a little bit of appliqué—all in good measure, so that no one task is too daunting.

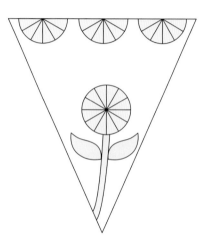

Materials and Supplies

Paper-piecing patterns are on pages CD105–CD108.

- **Off-white solid:** ½ yard for background and backs of half-circles

- **Solids (aqua, green, orange, pink, purple):** 1˝ × 10˝ strips of each for insert piecing

- **Print fabrics:** 1½˝ × 3˝ scraps, totaling ⅛ yard for circle and half-circles

- **Green-and-brown stripe:** 10˝ square for flower stem, leaves, and hanging tabs

- **Yellow rickrack, ½˝ wide:** 1¼ yards

- **Backing:** 1 fat quarter

- **Thin batting:** 18˝ × 21˝

- **½˝ bias pressing bar**

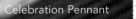

Cutting

OFF-WHITE SOLID

- 4 strips 4½˝ × 16˝ for insert pieced background

- 3 rectangles 3˝ × 5˝ for backs of foundation-pieced half-circles

SOLIDS

- 1 strip each 1˝ × 5˝ of green and purple

- 2 strips each 1˝ × 5˝ of aqua, orange, and pink

PRINTS

- 30 rectangles 1½˝ × 3˝

GREEN-AND-BROWN STRIPE

- Cut the 10˝ square in half on the bias to make 2 triangles. From the bias edge of each triangle, cut a 1½˝ strip (resulting in 2 strips each about 1½˝ × 14˝).

- 1 leaf and 1 reverse leaf using patterns on page CD108

YELLOW RICKRACK

- 3 pieces 8˝ for half-circles

- 1 piece 15˝ for circle

INSTRUCTIONS

All seam allowances are ¼˝.

Assemble the Insertion-Pieced Background

1. Cut a gentle angle across the short width of the off-white 4½˝ × 16˝ strip as shown. Sew a solid 1½˝ × 5˝ strip along the angled edge. Press the seam toward the strip.

2. Sew the other side of the inserted strip to the rest of the off-white strip. Press the seam toward the inserted strip. Add 2 more strips to the top row in the same manner.

DESIGN NOTE Refer to the finished project photo (page 135) for suggested placement of inserted solid strips. Keep in mind that the background strips will be sewn together and cut into a pennant triangle shape.

3. Insert 2 solid 1½˝ × 5˝ strips into each of 2 background strips and 1 solid strip into the remaining background strip.

4. Trim the background strips to 4˝ wide.

5. Stitch the background strips together. Press seams open.

6. Make a copy of the pennant triangle pattern (which includes seam allowance), lay it over the pieced background, trace around it, and cut out.

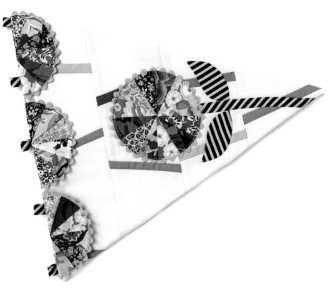

Assemble the Foundation-Pieced Half-Circle

1. Assemble 5 half-circles from the print 1½″ × 3″ rectangles. Trim ¼″ beyond all outside edges on the curved and straight edges.

2. Sew 2 half-circles together to make a circle. Press the seam open and remove the foundation papers.

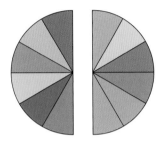

3. Align the long edges of the remaining pieced half-circles, right sides facing, with the off-white 3″ × 5″ rectangles. With a ¼″ seam allowance, stitch along the curved edge of the half-circles.

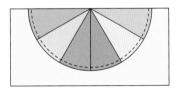

4. Trim the off-white solid even with the curved edges of the half-circles. Clip the seam allowance approximately every ¼″. Use a point turner to turn right sides out; press.

Attach the Rickrack Trim

1. Pin an 8″ strip of rickrack under the half-circles so that from the front you can see rickrack "bumps" along the curved edge. Edgestitch along the curved edge.

2. Place the rickrack on the right side of the full circle along the curve's raw edge. Keep the outer rickrack "bumps" even with the raw edge.

3. Fold approximately ⅜″ of the rickrack up (*not under*) at the beginning of the stitching line. Beginning at this folded edge, stitch down the center of the rickrack along the curved edge.

4. Overlap approximately ¼″ of rickrack over the folded beginning edge. The raw end will be on the top layer. Press the seam flat. Flip the rickrack to the back of the pieced circle and press.

Make the Bias Stem

1. Fold the 1½″ × 14″ bias strips in half along the length. Press.

2. Insert the ½″ bias pressing bar in the folded strip, wrong sides together. Keeping the bar even with the fold and moving it down the length of the strip as you sew, stitch right next to the pressing bar to create a ¼″ seam. Trim the seam to ⅛″.

3. Realign the seam so it is centered along the length of the pressing bar and press.

4. From one of the bias strips, cut 5 pieces 1½″ long. Fold these pieces in half widthwise and press. These are the hanging tabs for the top of the pennant.

5. From the remaining bias strip, cut a piece 6¼″ long. Place the strip near the bottom left corner of the pennant with raw edges aligned. Gently curve the strip and center it as it "grows" upward on the pennant. Pin or glue baste it in place. Hand or machine appliqué the stem in place.

Appliqué the Leaf and Flower

1. Hand or machine appliqué the leaves in place on either side of the stem, with the bottoms of the leaves approximately 5˝ from the pennant's bottom point.

2. Center the flower at the top of the stem, covering its raw edge. Edgestitch around the flower.

Assemble the Pennant

1. Fold the pennant in half lengthwise and mark the center.

2. Center a half-circle at the top of the pennant, with raw edges even. Pin in place.

3. Pin the remaining half-circles on either side of the center half-circle, taking care that the outer edges of the half-circles (including rickrack) will not be caught in the side seam allowance.

4. Sew along the top edge to baste the half-circles in place.

5. Add the pennant hanging tabs. With raw edges even, center a folded bias strip on top of the center pieced half-circle. Pin in place. Pin the remaining 4 folded tabs 2½˝ and 5˝ away from the center tab on either side. Baste in place.

6. Layer the pennant (right side up), backing fabric (right side down), and batting. Using the pennant shape as a guide, stitch all layers together, leaving a 4˝ opening on one side of the pennant triangle for turning.

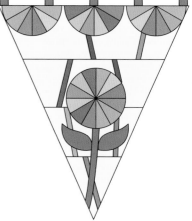

7. Trim the corners and seams near the corners. Turn right sides out using a point turner.

8. Press the hanging tabs up and the half-circles down at the top edge and hand stitch the opening closed.

ROLL-UP
Backgammon Board

FINISHED BOARD SIZE: 17½″ × 19″ • 17½″ × 26″, including pocket and flap

MADE BY Daniel Rouse

This backgammon board includes storage pockets for game pieces and rolls up for a trip to the beach or a walk to the park. But you may want to leave it out on the living room table to show off its many lovely details.

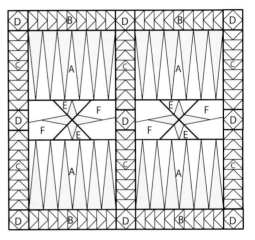

Materials and Supplies

Paper-piecing patterns are on pages CD109 and CD110.

- **Green print fabric 1:** 6½″ × 18″ for backgammon points

- **Contrasting green print fabric 2:** 6½″ × 18″ for backgammon points

- **Cream solid fabric:** 1⅛ yard for background

- **Blue print fabrics:** totaling ¼ yard for flying geese (I used 24 different prints.)

- **Green-and-blue print 1:** enough for 9 fussy-cut 2″ × 2″ squares

- **Green-and-blue print 2:** 1 fat eighth for accent stars

- **Green solid fabric:** 1 fat quarter for pocket

- **Green print fabric 3:** 18″ × 26½″ for cover

- **Blue solid fabric:** 2 strips 1½″ × 17″ for ties

- **Fusible fleece:** 18″ × 19½″

Cutting

GREEN PRINT 1 AND 2

- Cut each rectangle into 12 wedges ¾" wide at the top and 2" wide at the bottom for backgammon points.

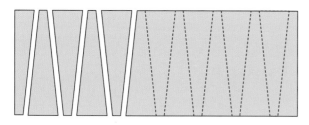

BLUE PRINT

- 84 rectangles 1½" × 2½" for Flying Geese

GREEN-AND-BLUE PRINT 1

- Fussy cut 9 squares 2" × 2" for border squares

GREEN-AND-BLUE PRINT 2

- 8 rectangles 1½" × 4" for stars

GREEN SOLID FABRIC

- 2 rectangles 4¼" × 18" for pocket

CREAM SOLID

- 6 strips 2¼" × 40". Subcut strips into 102 squares 2¼" × 2¼"; then cut squares diagonally into 204 triangles for borders.

- 1 strip 6½" × 40". Subcut strip into 28 wedges ¾" wide at the top and 2" wide at the bottom for backgammon points.

- 8 rectangles 2" × 2½" for stars

- 8 rectangles 2½" × 4½" for stars

- 2 strips 1" × 17" for side borders

- 2 strips 1" × 19½" for top and bottom borders

- 1 rectangle 8" × 18" for pocket flap

INSTRUCTIONS

All seam allowances are ¼".

Assemble the Backgammon Board

1. Assemble 4 section A blocks using the cream background wedges for the odd-numbered pieces and alternating green prints 1 and 2 for the backgammon points.

2. Assemble 4 section B blocks and 6 section C blocks using the blue print rectangles for the geese and the small cream background triangles.

3. Assemble 9 section D blocks using the fussy-cut green-and-blue print 1 and the small cream background triangles.

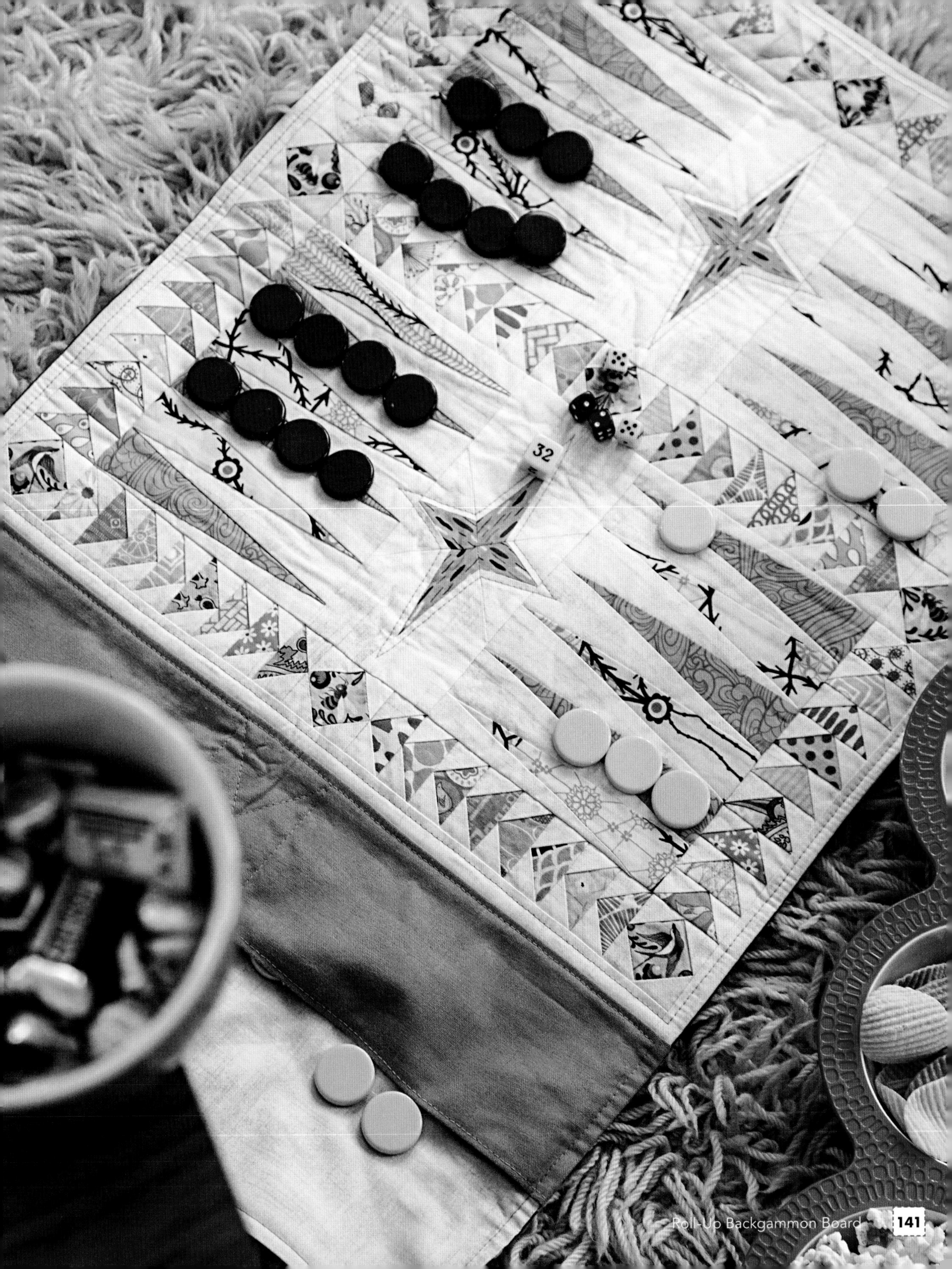
32

4. Arrange the A blocks so the backgammon points point downward. Sew a B block to the top of each A block. Make sure that for 2 blocks, the geese point right, and for the other 2 blocks, the geese point left.

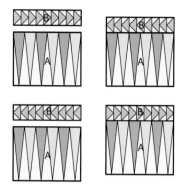

5. Make the outer edge DC strips by joining D to C to D to C to D so that the geese in each C block point toward the center D block. Repeat this step to make 2 strips.

6. Make the center DC strip by joining D to C to D to C to D so that the geese in each C block point away from the center D block.

7. Assemble 4 section E blocks using the green-and-blue print 2 and the 2″ × 2½″ cream background rectangles.

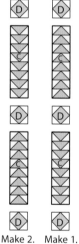

Make 2.   Make 1.

8. Assemble 4 section F blocks using the green-and-blue print 2 and the 2″ × 4½″ cream background rectangles.

9. Sew the E blocks to the slanted side of the F blocks, taking care to match the star points. Sew the EF blocks together in pairs as shown.

10. Sew an EF star between 2 AB blocks so that the backgammon points in each A block point toward the EF star and the geese in both B blocks point right. Sew an outer edge DC strip to the left of this strip.

11. Sew the other EF star between the remaining AB blocks so that the backgammon points in each A block point toward the EF star and the geese in both B blocks point left. Sew an outer edge DC strip to the right of this strip.

12. Sew the center DC strip between the star strips so the B geese point toward the DC strip.

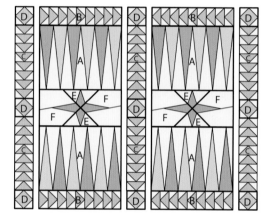

13. Pin and sew the cream 1″ × 17″ strips to the sides of the playing board and the cream 1″ × 19½″ strips to the top and bottom. Press seams toward the strips.

14. Remove all foundations from the wrong side of the playing board. Apply the fusible fleece to the wrong side of the playing board and quilt around the accent stars.

Assemble the Roll Tie

1. Fold under and press a short end of each blue tie strip by ¼″.

2. Press the strips in half lengthwise; open and press each long edge toward the middle to meet at the center crease. Fold in half again and topstitch around the edge to create 2 blue ⅜″ × 16¾″ ties.

Assemble the Pocket

1. Pin the pocket rectangles 4¼″ × 18″ right sides together and sew along a long edge. Press the seam open, fold wrong sides together, and press the seam flat. Topstitch the seam about ⅛″ from the edge.

2. Pin and sew the unsewn long edge of the pocket to one side of the backgammon board. Press the seam toward the backgammon board.

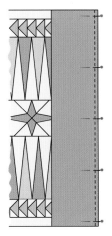

Assemble the Roll

1. Lay the large cover rectangle right side up on a table. Place the 2 ties on the cover 4½″ from the top and bottom long edges, with the unfinished tie ends hanging over the left edge by ¼″.

2. Place the backgammon board and pocket right side down, with the pocket to the right. Align the edge of the board with the left edge of the cover.

3. Align the 8″ × 18″ pocket flap rectangle right side down with the right side of the cover.

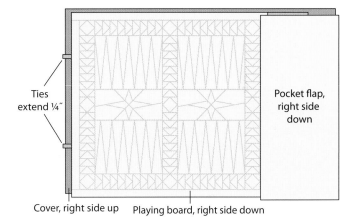

Ties extend ¼″

Pocket flap, right side down

Cover, right side up   Playing board, right side down

4. Pin, taking care to align the edges where multiple layers overlap, and secure the ties. Sew around the cover rectangle.

5. Clip the corners and turn right side out through the pocket flap gap. Press the edges flat.

6. Place the board right side up on a table. Ensure that the overlapping pocket layers are flat and straight. Pin along the base of the pocket.

7. Topstitch a rectangle around the backgammon board, about ¼″ from the edge of the pocket and the top, bottom, and left sides of the board.

8. Topstitch a second rectangle around the pocket flap, about ¼″ from the base of the pocket and the top, bottom, and right sides of the flap.

9. Topstitch a small rectangle and an "X" shape in the center of the pocket cover to create 2 pockets.

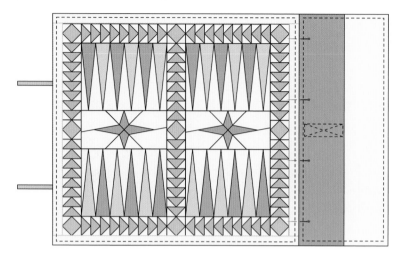

NOTE To roll the board for storage, place the backgammon pieces and dice in the two pockets and fold the flap over the pockets. Fold the board in half lengthwise, taking care to keep the pockets covered. Starting at the pocket end, roll up the board. Wrap the ties around the board and tie.

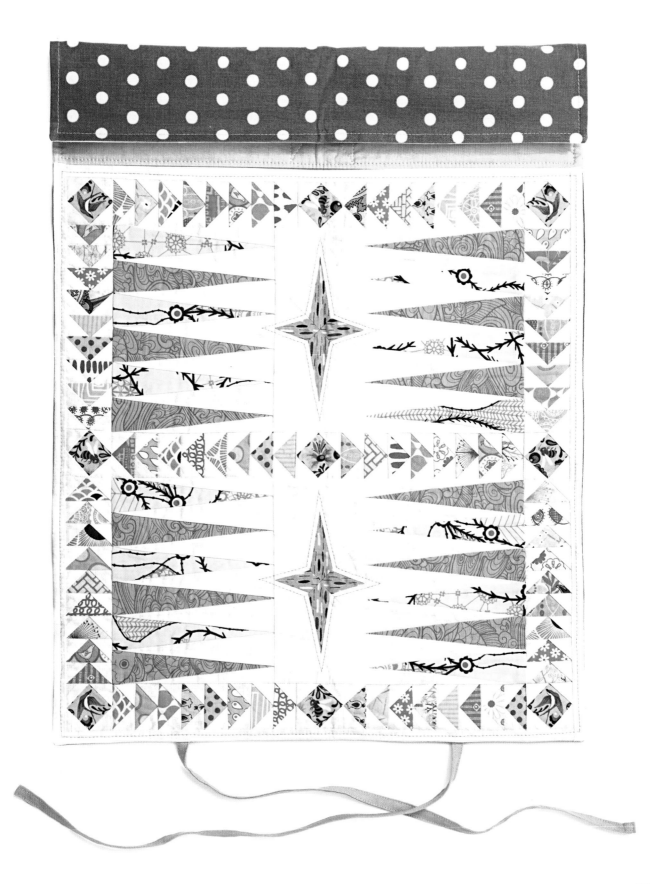

Roll-Up Backgammon Board **145**

Kid's Book Bag

FINISHED BLOCK SIZE (each paper clip): 6″ × 6″ • FINISHED BAG SIZE: 14″ × 17″

MADE BY Laura Jane Taylor

This tote bag with fabric dividers is perfect for organizing your child's reading books. Have fun thinking up personalized labels to suit your little bookworm!

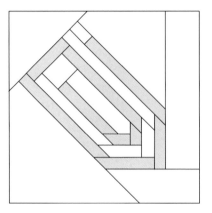

Materials and Supplies

Paper-piecing patterns are on page CD111.

- **White text fabric:** ½ yard for background of paper clip blocks
- **4 colors of assorted scraps:** less than ¼ yard each for paper clip blocks
- **Dark gray fabric:** ⅛ yard for inner border
- **Aqua fabric:** ¼ yard for outer border
- **Gray fabric:** 1 fat quarter for back of bag
- **White newsprint fabric:** ½ yard for bag lining
- **Orange fabric:** ½ yard for dividers

- **Yellow fabric:** ½ yard for dividers
- **Green fabric:** ½ yard for dividers
- **Medium-weight fusible interfacing:** 1 yard if interfacing is 35″ wide, or 2 yards if using 18″-wide interfacing
- **1″-wide cotton twill tape:** 2 yards
- **Erasable fabric pen**
- **Small alphabet stamps and fabric ink pad** *OR* **permanent fabric pen**

DARK GRAY

- 2 strips 1″ × 12½″ for inner border
- 2 strips 1″ × 13½″ for inner border

AQUA

- 2 strips 2½″ × 13½″ for outer border
- 2 strips 2½″ × 17½″ for outer border

GRAY

- 1 square 17½″ × 17½″ for back of bag

WHITE NEWSPRINT

- 2 squares 17½″ × 17½″ for lining

ORANGE

- 2 pieces 13″ × 14½″ for fabric dividers

YELLOW

- 2 pieces 13″ × 14½″ for fabric dividers

GREEN

- 2 pieces 13″ × 14½″ for fabric dividers

COTTON TWILL TAPE

- 3 pieces 1″ × 2½″ for labels
- 2 pieces 1″ × 25″ for labels

INTERFACING

- 4 pieces 17½″ × 17½″

INSTRUCTIONS

All seam allowances are ¼″.

Assemble the Block

1. Assemble 4 paper clip blocks using the white text print fabric for the background and each of the colors for the paper clips. Trim each block to 6½″ × 6½″.

NOTE Pieces 15 and 16 must be joined before sewing to the foundation. Cut a 1″ × 4½″ strip of colored fabric for piece 15 and a 1″ × 1½″ strip of text fabric for piece 16. Sew together end to end, right sides together and press the seam open. Make sure the seam aligns with the printed seamline on the foundation; then, stitch in place.

2. Sew the 4 paper clip blocks together as shown.

Assemble the Outer Bag

1. Sew the dark gray 1″ × 12½″ strips to the sides of the paper clip block, and sew the dark gray 1″ × 13½″ strips to the top and bottom. Press seams toward the strips.

2. Sew the aqua 2½″ × 13½″ strips to the sides of the paper clip block, and sew the aqua 2½″ × 17½″ strips to the top and bottom. Press seams toward the strips.

3. Remove the paper foundations. Apply the fusible interfacing to the front and back of the bag and to the 2 lining pieces.

4. Sew the bag front and back together on 3 sides, right sides together. Leave the top of the bag open.

Make the Dividers

1. Print words such as "READING," "HOMEWORK," and "JUST FOR FUN" on the top half of the 3 twill 1″ × 2½″ strips. Leave at least ¼″ free space at the bottom of the tape for the seam allowance.

------------------- **TIP** -------------------

You could also use a fabric marker to write the labels.

2. Fold a fabric divider piece in half along the 14½″ side. Mark the center with a crease.

3. With the divider piece right side up, place a twill tape label upside down and facing down. The bottom of the twill tape should be at the edge of the divider at the center point marked in Step 2.

14½″

4. Pin the second divider piece on the first, right sides together and long sides matching. Sew along the top, making sure to trap the label in the seam. Pin and sew along the bottom.

5. Turn the divider right side out and press. Topstitch along the top, ⅛″ away from the edge.

6. Repeat Steps 2–5 for the next divider, positioning the label 3″ to the left of center.

7. Repeat Steps 2–5 for the last divider, positioning the label 3″ to the right of center.

Make the Lining

1. Stack the 3 fabric dividers in the order they will appear in the bag, and pin together.

2. Place a lining piece right side up. Measure and mark 1½″ down from the top edge on both side edges, using an erasable fabric marker. Position the dividers on top of the lining so that the top left corner meets the left-side mark and all pieces are aligned along the left edge. Pin in place. Note that the fabric dividers won't reach either the bottom or the mark on the right side.

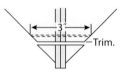

3. Place the second lining piece on top of the first, right sides together, aligning all edges. Pin securely through all 5 layers and stitch down the left edge. Flip back the top layer of the lining.

4. Match the top right corner of all dividers to the right mark on the lining, and align the lining and fabric dividers along the right side. Flip the top layer back in place, pin, and stitch along the right side. The fabric dividers will not reach all the way across the lining—they will hang as if suspended from the sides.

5. Sew across the bottom of the lining, leaving a 5″ gap in the middle for turning. Backstitch at both edges of the gap.

Box the Corners

1. Turn the bag inside out. To create a box corner, make a triangle at the bottom by centering the left-side seam over the bottom seam. Flatten the sides evenly and draw a 3″ line across the corner. Stitch along this line. Stitch again to reinforce the seam. Trim off the excess, leaving a ¼″ seam allowance.

2. Repeat Step 1 for the bottom right side of the bag. Make box corners for the lining. Press all pieces.

Finish the Bag

1. Find the center front of the bag opening and mark 2½″ on both sides. Pin the ends of one of the 25″ handles at the marks. Take care not to twist the handle when pinning.

2. Repeat Step 1 for the back of the bag and the second handle.

3. Turn the lining wrong side out. Place the bag inside the lining, right sides together. Match the side seams and pin around the bag's top edge. Sew the bag and lining together, securing the handle ends but making sure the handle loops and dividers are out of the way.

4. Turn the bag right side out and machine stitch the opening closed.

5. Push the lining and dividers into the bag and press well to smooth out the seam at the top edge. Topstitch around the bag's entire top edge.

The Old Clock Quilt
LONDON TIME

MADE BY Lynne Goldsworthy • **FINISHED QUILT SIZE: 54″ × 54″**

Don't you sometimes wish time would stand still? Wouldn't it be nice to capture those rare moments when everyone is happy and all the work for the day is done? This stylish, classic clock quilt can do just that. Set the time on the clock to that special moment and place where you were happiest. The plaid is by Denyse Schmidt for Freespirit, the cream grunge fabric is by BasicGrey for Moda, the charcoal sketch fabric is from Timeless Treasures, and the black solid is by Oakshott.

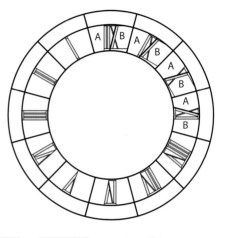

Materials and Supplies

Paper-piecing patterns are on pages CD112–CD126.

- **Cream fabric:** 1½ yards for clock face background

- **Charcoal fabric:** ½ yard for Roman numerals and "LONDON TIME"

- **Black solid fabric:** ½ yard for clock frame

- **Black plaid fabric:** 3⅛ yards for wall (If your plaid is larger, get enough to match the plaid.)

- **Backing fabric:** 3½ yards

- **Binding fabric:** ½ yard

- **Batting:** 62″ × 62″

- **Fusible web:** approximately 10″ × 20″

CREAM GRUNGE FABRIC

- 1 strip 1″ × width of fabric; subcut into 8 strips 1″ × 3½″ to sash the words

- 1 strip 3½″ × width of fabric; subcut into 2 strips 3½″ × 9¼″ and 2 strips 3½″ × 6½″ to sash the words

- 3 strips 7½″ × 27″ for clock face

- Use the remainder to piece the Roman numerals and letters.

BLACK SOLID FABRIC

- 12 pieces using clock frame pattern on page CD124

BLACK PLAID FABRIC

- 2 pieces 58″ × width of fabric for wall

BACKING FABRIC

- 2 pieces 62″ × width of fabric

BINDING FABRIC:

- 6 strips 2½″ × width of fabric

INSTRUCTIONS

Note: All seam allowances are ¼″.

Assemble the Roman Numerals

1. Assemble Roman numerals 1–8.

2. For Roman numerals 9, 10, 11, and 12, assemble sections A and B and join to create each Roman numeral.

3. Join the Roman numerals at the side seams to make a ring. Press the seams counterclockwise.

Assemble the Clock Face Center

1. Assemble the letters for the words "LONDON" and "TIME." Trim the letter "I" to 1″ × 3½″. Trim the letter "M" to 3½″ × 3½″. Trim all other letters to 2½″ × 3½″.

2. Use the cream 1″ × 3½″ strips between the letters to form "LONDON" and "TIME."

3. Sew a cream 3½″ × 6½″ strip to both ends of "LONDON." Repeat for "TIME," using the cream 3½″ × 9¼″ strips.

4. Sew a cream 7½″ × 27″ strip between "LONDON" and "TIME."

5. Sew the remaining cream 7½″ × 27″ strips to the top and bottom of the "LONDON TIME" piece.

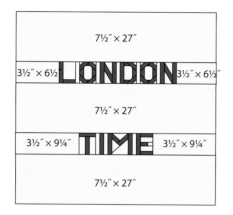

Attach the Roman Numerals to the Clock Face

1. Fold the clock face in half horizontally and vertically to find the center top, center bottom, and center of both sides. Fold the Roman numeral ring to find its centers at the top, bottom, and sides.

2. Pin the ring to the clock face, right sides together, first matching center marks, then at each seam and several places in between. Before sewing, check that the ring is centered on the square. Sew with the Roman numeral ring on top and the clock face underneath.

3. Press the seam toward the ring. Trim the clock face into a circle.

Assemble the Clock Frame

1. Sew the 12 clock frame sections together to make a ring. Press the seams counterclockwise.

2. Pin the clock frame to the Roman numerals, right sides together, at every seam and in several places in between. Sew together with the clock frame on top and the Roman numerals underneath. Press the seam toward the clock frame.

Assemble the Wall

1. Sew the 2 plaid 58″ × width of fabric pieces together along the 58″ edges, aligning the plaid pattern if needed. Trim to 54″ square.

2. Center the clock face on the wrong side of the wall fabric and trace around it. Draw a second circle ½″ smaller than the first circle inside the traced clock face and cut out. (You can use the circle for another project.)

3. Pin the wall to the clock, right sides together, at every seam and in several places in between. Sew together with the wall fabric on top and the clock underneath. Press the seam toward the wall fabric.

Add the Clock Center and Hands

1. Cut out the patterns for the hour and minute hands, and tape together.

2. Trace the clock hands and the central circle pattern onto the fusible web. Cut them out roughly and fuse to the back of the clock hand fabric.

3. Carefully cut out the hands and fuse them, followed by the center circle, to the quilt.

4. Sew around the edges of the hands and circle using a blanket, zigzag, or other decorative stitch.

Finish the Quilt

1. Remove the foundations. Layer the backing, batting, and quilt top. Quilt as desired. (I quilted using a cross hatch with diagonal lines 1˝ apart using Aurifil 50wt 2326.)

2. Sew the binding strips end to end using diagonal joining seams. Press in half along the length. Machine sew the strips to the front of the quilt, mitering the corners. Hand sew the binding to the back to finish the quilt.

The Contributors

THE COMPILER

TACHA BRUECHER is a quilt designer and teacher and is well known in the online quilting community as a founding member of Fat Quarterly e-magazine. Her book *Hexa-go-go,* also published by Stash Books, takes a detailed look at English paper piecing and, more specifically, at how to incorporate hexagons into modern quilt designs.

Tacha has published many patterns and articles as a part of Fat Quarterly. She has also co-authored The Fat Quarterly Shape Workshop for Quilters. Her patterns have appeared in a number of other publications, including *Modern Blocks* (Stash Books), *Pillow Pop* (Stash Books), and *Mollie Makes.*

Tacha dabbled in many crafts before discovering her love of quilting, when she became hooked. The world of Flickr swaps and online bees have only served to heighten her obsession with fabric. She is now rarely to be found without thread or fabric in her hands (or on her clothes!).

ALSO BY TACHA BRUECHER:

Flickr: *flickr.com/photos/snuggledown* • Blog: *haniesquilts.blogspot.com*
Twitter: *twitter.com/hanies1* • Website: *fatquarterly.com*

THE ARTISTS

CHERYL ARKISON is a writer, quilter, and mom. Her quilts and articles have appeared in numerous print and online publications. From her crowded, colorful house, she wrote her books, *Sunday Morning Quilts* (co-authored with Amanda Jean Nyberg) and *A Month of Sundays* (Stash Books). She is the mother of three kidlets and blogs regularly on Dining Room Empire.

Blog: *naptimequilter.blogspot.com* • Website: *cherylarkison.com*

LEILA BEASLEY was taught to sew by her mum. It wasn't until she stumbled upon modern quilting blogs in 2010 that she began to enjoy quilts. Once Leila discovered paper piecing and Japanese zakka-style patchwork, she became inspired and hasn't stopped sewing since! Leila creates pretty things for everyday use and runs a shop online where you can find her handmade zakka goods and paper-piecing patterns.

Blog: *wheretheorchidsgrow.blogspot.com* • Website: *wheretheorchidsgrow.etsy.com*

SONJA CALLAGHAN is from Vancouver, British Columbia, Canada. Designing quilt patterns is her obsession. She's been designing for about six years and has been in collaboration with *Quiltmaker Magazine*, designing kid-themed paper-pieced patterns. You can keep up with her new patterns, read fun tidbits about the modern quilt scene in the northwest coast, find tutorials, and even snag free patterns on her blog.

Blog: *Artisania.ca*

MEGAN DYE is a fabric-obsessed mom of two in Portland, Oregon. Her lifelong love of crafting has developed into a passion for design. As a self-taught sewist, she appreciates the generous and inspiring bloggers and crafters online. Writing clear, easy-to-follow tutorials is one way she gives back to that community. Megan also enjoys crafting for a cause and donates 100 percent of her shop's proceeds to charity.

Blog: *megsmonkeybeans.blogspot.com* • Website: *megsmonkeybeans.etsy.com*

AMY FRIEND enjoys designing, quilting, sewing, and printmaking. She has been blogging about her creations since 2009. Her work as a fine art collections curator provided her with the opportunity to examine art on a daily basis. While raising her three children, she has focused her creative energy on sewing. She designs for BasicGrey, Sizzix, and the Art Gallery Fat Quarter Gang, as well as independently selling items in her Etsy and Craftsy shops.

Blog: *duringquiettime.com* • Website: *duringquiettime.etsy.com*

JULIANNA GASIOROWSKA is a hardworking mother and wife trying to find free time for her patchwork passion. She lives in beautiful Warsaw (Poland), a city with no local quilt shops. When Julianna was pregnant, she discovered online shops selling gorgeous modern fabrics. Now Julianna's idea of the perfect evening is one spent in her creative space. You can "meet" Julianna at her blog and on Flickr.

Flickr: *flickr.com/photos/jednoiglec* • Blog: *sewingunderrainbow.com*

LYNNE GOLDSWORTHY's interest in quilting took off after she discovered modern fabrics and online communities. Lynne is co-author of *500 Quilt Blocks* (Search Press) and her patterns have been published in a variety of books, including *Modern Blocks* (Stash Books). She helps run the modern online quilting e-zine Fat Quarterly and hosts the annual Fat Quarterly Sewing Retreat in London. Lynne lives in the United Kingdom with her four children, two cats, and a long-suffering Welsh husband.

Blog: *lilysquilts.blogspot.com* • Website: *fatquarterly.com*

KERRY GREEN loves thrifty finds, vintage fabric, and kitchenalia. Kerry quilts, makes purses, and sews clothing—she wants to do it all! Kerry shares tips, patterns, and tutorials at her blog. Through the online quilting community, Kerry met Penny Layman, and together they formed Sew-Ichigo, where they combine graphic, vintage-inspired ideas to make paper-piecing patterns and quilt blocks. Kerry is also co-author of *500 Quilt Blocks* published by Search Press.

Blogs: *verykerryberry.blogspot.com* • *sew-ichigo.blogspot.com*

PENNY LAYMAN is a quilter and designer living in Colorado with her husband and cat. Her love for paper piecing was born about two years ago; since then, she hasn't looked back. Penny also teaches classes on how to paper piece and design paper-piecing patterns. Please email her at sewtakeahike@gmail.com with workshop and class inquiries. Penny's patterns have been published in a number of books, including *Modern Blocks* and *Pillow Pop*, both published by Stash Books.

Blogs: *sewtakeahike.typepad.com* • *sew-ichigo.blogspot.com*
Website: *etsy.com/shop/sewtakeahike*

AMY LOBSIGER has been quilting for twenty years and blogging about it since 2007. She is fond of projects that combine techniques for an eclectic finish. Her fabric tastes run the gamut as well, and you will readily find her combining Kaffe Fassett with Civil War prints. Fabric combinations depend on what she is looking for but can't find in her vast stash. You can find tutorials at her blog and doll quilt patterns for sale through Dollies Online, a monthly program that Amy runs with her friend Sarah Fielke.

Blog: *mrsschmenkmanquilts.wordpress.com*
Website: *sarahfielke.com/products/DolliesOnline*

TAMIKO PERCELL has been passionate about crafty endeavors for as long as she can remember. She was fortunate to grow up in a creative family and credits her mother and grandmother for her love of all things handmade. She discovered quilting two years ago and tries to push her creative and technical limits with each new project. Born and raised in Canada, Tamiko now resides in California with her wacky husband and fluffy cat. She wishes for a second cat.

Blog: *patchworknotes.blogspot.com*

ANGELA PINGEL is a self-taught quilter who has been sewing for more than twenty years. She made her first quilt in high school for her college dorm room. Recently the winner of the Moda Bakeshop Sliced Competition, she is also part of the Moda Bakeshop book, *Sweet Celebrations*. Angela has been published in *101 Patchwork Projects*, *Modern Patchwork*, and *Quilt Scene* (Interweave Press); *99 Modern Blocks* (Stash); and *Quiltmaker's 100 Blocks*. She manages her blog in her free time between sewing and raising her sweet little girl with her husband.

Blogs: *cuttopieces.blogspot.com* • *sew-ichigo.blogspot.com*

CAROLINE M. PRESS designs purses and other sewn goods based out of her Corvallis, Oregon, studio. She believes in attention to detail with a practical aesthetic that is reflected in her work. She has authored work in Fat Quarterly e-zine and enjoys a strong web presence in the crafting community. She blogs about her sewing and knitting escapades, and offers some free foundation-piecing patterns online. Her purse patterns are available for sale through Craftsy, her blog, and her Etsy shop.

Blog: *trilliumdesign.blogspot.com* • Website: *etsy.com/shop/trilliumshoppe*

CHARISE RANDELL has designed apparel for twenty years for clients such as Nordstrom, Eddie Bauer, and Union Bay. Her recent work with paper piecing and quilting began when she was invited to join a quilting bee. Her style is inspired by vintage domestic arts and the beauty of simple craft. You can find her apparel, quilt, and accessory designs in *Stitch* and *Quiltmaker* magazines, as well as her patterns and tutorials on her blog. Charise lives in Seattle with her husband and two sons.

Blog: *charisecreates.blogspot.com* • Email: *charise_randell@yahoo.com*
Websites: *etsy.com/shop/ChariseCreates* • *craftsy.com/user/654996/pattern-store*

DANIEL ROUSE has a professional background in landscape architecture and has the same goals in designing for landscape and fabric—to create an experience using composition, materials, movement, and surprise. His bold, graphic quilts draw on traditional, contemporary, and modern approaches. He gravitates toward large quilts, but loves to experiment with new techniques on small projects. Daniel enjoys teaching quilting and never fails to learn something new from each bunch of students.

Blog: *pieceandpress.blogspot.com*

KYLIE SELDON was taught to sew as a child by her mum and has always enjoyed making things. She has dabbled in many creative arenas and loves learning new crafty skills. Kylie recently discovered patchwork via the wonderful online crafting community and enjoys designing and making paper-pieced quilt blocks and zakka-style patchwork projects. She is particularly inspired by Japanese fabrics and patchwork styles. Kylie lives in Australia with her wonderful husband and three children.

Blog: *three-honeybees.blogspot.com.au*

AYUMI TAKAHASHI discovered her love of paper piecing when she started the Ringo Pie bee with Penny Layman and other talented friends in 2010. She loves that paper piecing results in precise-looking projects, no matter how sloppy the fabric pieces were cut. She is the author of *Patchwork Please* (Interweave Press) and has collaborated with Superbuzzy on the Super Penguin Quilt Along. (You can find the block patterns on Superbuzzy.com.) She moved from the United States to Tokyo in 2011 to be near her family and friends.

Blog: *ayumills.blogspot.com*

LAURA JANE TAYLOR strives to create innovative and beautiful modern quilts in the sea of oh-so-beautiful quilts already out there. She knits, she sews, she quilts, and she blogs. It's who she is. Needles, Pins, and Baking Tins is where Laura writes about whatever she is working on—quilts she's stitching up, swaps she's involved in, trips she's planning, photos she's taken, and the general comings and goings of a quilt-crazed twenty-something living in middle England with a couple of cats.

Blog: *needlespinsandbakingtins.com*

JOANNA WILCZYNSKA finished her first quilt in 2010. She started to design patterns, and publish her projects. She uses various techniques to create a unique look, including traditional piecing, paper piecing, embroidery, fabric painting, and free-motion quilting. Seeking new challenges, in 2011 she made her first art quilt, *Among the Red Flowers*, which won multiple international prizes.

Blog: *shape-moth.blogspot.de*

CHASE WU is currently earning her master's in fine arts degree in mixed media and focusing on fiber art. She finds time between school and work to sew and craft. Chase enjoys every process of sewing and uses photography to document each sewing project at her blog, where she shares sewing tutorials and features of weekend life with her daughter.

Blog: *quarterinchmark.blogspot.com*

Resources

FABRICS
Robert Kaufman Fabrics
robertkaufman.com

Moda Fabrics
unitednotions.com

Liberty Lifestyle Fabrics
liberty.co.uk > Fabric

Windham Fabrics
windhamfabrics.com

Oakshott Fabrics
www.oakshottfabrics.com

RECOMMENDED RETAILERS
Fat Quarter Shop
fatquartershop.com

eQuilter
equilter.com

SUPPLIES
Aurifil
aurifil.com

Electric Quilt Company
electricquilt.com

Sizzix
sizzix.com

LONGARM QUILTING
Angela Walters
quiltingismytherapy.com

ONLINE PAPER-PIECING RESOURCES
Sew-Ichigo
sew-ichigo.blogspot.com

Y-seams
charisecreates.blogspot.com > Tutorials > Y Seams Tutorial

patchworknotes.blogspot.com

Embroidery Stitches
iPhone and Android app

Judith Baker Montano's Embroidery & Crazy Quilt Stitch Guide